Introduction

What does it mean to be progressive?

In an age of political polarization and oversimplified labels, this book aims to clarify the philosophy, history, and goals behind progressive thought. *On Being Progressive* is not a partisan manifesto, but a guide to understanding a worldview rooted in equity, justice, sustainability, and human dignity.

By exploring topics ranging from economic inequality to environmental activism, this book offers a broad yet accessible look at how progressivism differs from conservatism—and why those differences matter.Whether you're a committed progressive, a curious observer, or simply seeking perspective, I invite you to walk this path with clarity and purpose.

Rick Rossi

August 2024

Table of Contents

What It Means to Be a Political Progressive

Defining Progressivism

Political progressivism is a movement or ideology that advocates for social reform, aiming to address inequalities and injustices in society through government action and public policy. Progressives believe in the potential for change and improvement in society and see the government as a key player in driving that change. This ideology has deep roots in history, often arising during periods of social and economic upheaval when existing systems are perceived as inadequate or unjust.

Progressives typically advocate for a wide range of issues, from economic equality and social justice to environmental sustainability and democratic reforms. The core belief is that society can and should be improved through collective efforts, with a focus on addressing systemic problems that affect marginalized or disadvantaged groups.

Core Principles of Progressivism

1. **Social Justice**: Progressives are committed to reducing social inequalities, whether based on race, gender, class, or other factors. This includes supporting policies that promote equal

opportunities, combat discrimination, and provide for the needs of those who are economically or socially disadvantaged. Social justice also extends to advocating for the rights of marginalized groups, such as LGBTQ+ individuals, immigrants, and racial minorities.

2. **Economic Equality**: A key tenet of progressivism is the belief that economic systems should work for everyone, not just the wealthy or powerful. Progressives often support policies that redistribute wealth, such as progressive taxation, a higher minimum wage, and stronger social safety nets. They argue that these measures are necessary to address the growing income inequality and to ensure that all members of society have access to basic needs like healthcare, education, and housing.

3. **Environmental Sustainability**: Progressives are often at the forefront of environmental advocacy, pushing for policies that protect the planet and ensure that future generations can enjoy a healthy environment. This includes supporting renewable energy sources, reducing carbon emissions, and implementing regulations to curb pollution. For progressives, environmental sustainability is closely linked to social justice, as environmental

degradation often disproportionately affects marginalized communities.

4. **Democratic Reforms**: Progressives typically believe in strengthening democratic institutions and ensuring that the government is accountable to the people. This can involve advocating for campaign finance reform, expanding voting rights, and fighting against gerrymandering. Progressives often support increasing transparency in government and reducing the influence of money in politics to create a more equitable and representative democracy.

5. **Human Rights and Civil Liberties**: Progressives champion human rights and civil liberties, advocating for the protection and expansion of these rights both domestically and internationally. This includes supporting policies that protect freedom of speech, privacy, and due process, as well as opposing government overreach and authoritarianism. Progressives also often advocate for the rights of workers, believing that everyone should have the right to fair wages, safe working conditions, and the ability to organize,

Historical Context of Progressivism

The roots of modern progressivism can be traced back to the late 19th and early 20th centuries during the Progressive Era in the United States. During this time, reformers sought to address the problems created by industrialization, urbanization, and political corruption. They pushed for reforms such as child labor laws, women's suffrage, and antitrust legislation, laying the groundwork for many of the issues that progressives continue to champion today.

Over time, progressivism has evolved, adapting to the changing social and political landscape. The civil rights movement of the 1950s and 1960s, for example, was deeply influenced by progressive ideals, as were the feminist and environmental movements of the 1970s. In recent years, progressivism has gained renewed prominence as a response to growing economic inequality, climate change, and social injustice.

Modern Progressive Movements

In contemporary politics, progressivism is often associated with left-leaning political parties and movements that seek to challenge the status quo. This can be seen in the rise of figures like Bernie Sanders and Alexandria Ocasio-Cortez in the United States, who have championed progressive policies such as Medicare for All, tuition-free college, and the Green New Deal. These leaders and their supporters advocate for a more equitable and just society, often in opposition to neoliberal or conservative policies that prioritize free markets and limited government intervention.

Internationally, progressive movements can be found in many countries, often focusing on similar issues of economic justice, environmental sustainability, and human rights. These movements frequently collaborate across borders, sharing ideas and strategies to address global challenges such as climate change, inequality, and the erosion of democratic norms.

Criticisms and Challenges

Progressivism is not without its critics. Some argue that progressive policies can be overly idealistic, leading to unintended consequences or economic inefficiencies. Others contend that progressivism can be too focused on government intervention, potentially stifling individual freedoms or innovation. Additionally, progressives often face opposition from conservative and centrist forces, who may see their policies as too radical or disruptive to existing systems.

Despite these challenges, progressivism remains a powerful force in modern politics, driven by a belief in the potential for positive change and a commitment to addressing the pressing issues of our time. For progressives, the goal is not just to resist or react to current problems, but to actively work toward creating a more just, equitable, and sustainable world. This vision of progress continues to inspire and mobilize people around the globe, making progressivism a dynamic and evolving ideology in the 21st century.

What It Means to Be a Political Conservative

Defining Conservatism

Political conservatism is a philosophy and movement that emphasizes the preservation of traditional institutions, values, and social structures. Conservatives often advocate for maintaining established norms and are cautious about rapid change or innovation, particularly in social and political realms. This ideology is rooted in a belief that longstanding institutions and practices have been shaped by collective wisdom and should be preserved to maintain social stability and order.

Conservatives tend to emphasize individual responsibility, limited government, free markets, and a strong national defense. While the specific priorities and policies of conservatives may vary across different cultures and historical periods, the core tenets of conservatism remain focused on preserving the social order, promoting economic freedom, and upholding moral values derived from tradition and religion.

Core Principles of Conservatism

1. **Tradition and Stability**: Conservatives place a high value on tradition, believing that long-standing customs and institutions provide a foundation for

a stable and orderly society. This respect for tradition is often linked to a belief in the importance of cultural continuity and the preservation of societal norms that have been passed down through generations. Conservatives argue that these traditions are essential for maintaining social cohesion and that sudden or radical changes can lead to disorder and instability.

2. **Limited Government**: A fundamental principle of conservatism is the belief in a limited role for government in the lives of individuals. Conservatives argue that government should focus on its core functions, such as maintaining law and order, protecting property rights, and defending the nation. They are often skeptical of large-scale government interventions in the economy or society, believing that such interventions can lead to inefficiency, dependency, and a loss of individual freedoms. Instead, conservatives advocate for free markets, private enterprise, and personal responsibility as the best means of ensuring prosperity and social well-being.

3. **Economic Freedom**: Conservatives are strong proponents of free-market capitalism, arguing that economic freedom is essential for individual

liberty and prosperity. They believe that markets, when left relatively free from government interference, are the most efficient way to allocate resources and create wealth. This belief in economic freedom often leads conservatives to oppose high taxes, excessive regulation, and government-run programs, favoring instead policies that promote entrepreneurship, competition, and private ownership.

4. **Moral and Religious Values**: Conservatism is often closely associated with a commitment to moral and religious values, which are seen as essential to the health of society. Many conservatives believe that these values, often rooted in Judeo-Christian traditions, provide a moral compass that guides behavior and promotes social order. As a result, conservatives often advocate for policies that align with traditional moral values, such as opposition to abortion, support for traditional marriage, and the promotion of religious freedom. They argue that a strong moral foundation is necessary for a thriving society and that the erosion of these values can lead to social decay.

5. **Nationalism and Patriotism**: Conservatives typically place a strong emphasis on national sovereignty, patriotism, and the protection of

national interests. They believe in the importance of maintaining a strong national defense and are often skeptical of international organizations or agreements that they perceive as compromising national autonomy. This focus on nationalism is often coupled with a belief in American exceptionalism, the idea that the United States has a unique role to play in the world as a beacon of freedom and democracy.

Historical Context of Conservatism

Conservatism as a distinct political philosophy emerged in response to the radical changes brought about by the Enlightenment and the French Revolution. Early conservatives, such as Edmund Burke, reacted against what they saw as the excessive rationalism and revolutionary fervor of the time, arguing instead for the preservation of traditional institutions, such as the monarchy, the church, and the family. They believed that these institutions were the product of accumulated wisdom and that radical change could lead to chaos and tyranny.

In the United States, conservatism developed as a response to the perceived threats of socialism, communism, and the expansion of federal government power. The modern conservative movement in the U.S.

gained momentum in the mid-20th century, particularly with the rise of figures like Barry Goldwater and Ronald Reagan. These leaders championed a brand of conservatism that emphasized limited government, free-market economics, and a strong anti-communist stance, which came to define American conservatism in the latter half of the 20th century.

Modern Conservative Movements

Today, political conservatism encompasses a broad range of movements and ideologies, from traditionalists who emphasize the preservation of cultural and religious values to libertarians who advocate for minimal government intervention in both the economy and personal lives. Despite these differences, contemporary conservatives generally share a commitment to the principles of limited government, free markets, and a strong national defense.

In the United States, the conservative movement is most closely associated with the Republican Party, which has championed conservative policies such as tax cuts, deregulation, and a strong military. However, conservatism is not monolithic, and there are significant differences within the movement. For example, some conservatives prioritize social issues, such as opposition to abortion and same-sex marriage, while others focus more on economic issues, such as reducing the size of government and lowering taxes.

Internationally, conservative movements vary widely depending on the historical and cultural context. In Europe, for instance, conservatism often includes a greater emphasis on social welfare and a more cautious approach to economic liberalization than in the United States. However, the core principles of preserving tradition, advocating for limited government, and emphasizing national sovereignty are common threads across conservative movements worldwide.

Criticisms and Challenges

Like any political ideology, conservatism faces criticism and challenges. Critics often argue that conservatism can be resistant to necessary social change, potentially perpetuating inequalities or outdated social norms. Others contend that conservative economic policies, such as tax cuts and deregulation, disproportionately benefit the wealthy and can exacerbate economic inequality.

Additionally, conservatism's emphasis on tradition and national sovereignty can sometimes lead to tensions with more progressive or globalist perspectives, particularly on issues such as immigration, climate change, and human rights. Conservatives are also sometimes criticized for prioritizing order and stability over social justice or for being too closely aligned with corporate interests.

Despite these criticisms, conservatism remains a powerful and influential force in global politics. Its emphasis on preserving established institutions, promoting individual responsibility, and maintaining a strong national defense continues to resonate with many people, particularly in times of social or economic uncertainty. For conservatives, the goal is not to resist change entirely but to ensure that any changes are measured, thoughtful, and grounded in respect for tradition and the wisdom of the past.

The Psychology of Progressive vs. Conservative Personalities

Overview of Political Personality Differences

Political orientation is often influenced by deeper psychological traits, with progressives and conservatives exhibiting distinct patterns in personality, values, and cognitive styles. These differences are not merely a matter of policy preference but are rooted in fundamental psychological processes that shape how individuals perceive the world, evaluate information, and make decisions.

Understanding these psychological underpinnings helps explain why individuals gravitate toward certain political ideologies and why these ideologies resonate with different aspects of human experience. This section explores the psychological traits commonly associated with progressive and conservative personalities, examining how these traits influence political behavior and attitudes.

Cognitive Styles and Openness to Experience

One of the most well-documented differences between progressives and conservatives lies in their cognitive styles, particularly in relation to the personality trait known as **openness to experience**.

- **Progressive Personalities**: Progressives tend to score higher on openness to experience, a trait associated with curiosity, creativity, and a willingness to engage with new ideas, experiences, and cultural diversity. This openness leads progressives to embrace change and innovation, making them more receptive to policies that challenge the status quo or seek to reform existing social and political structures. They are generally more comfortable with ambiguity and complexity, and they tend to be more tolerant of differences in values, lifestyles, and beliefs.

- **Conservative Personalities**: Conservatives, on the other hand, tend to score lower on openness to experience and higher on traits like **conscientiousness**, which is associated with a preference for order, structure, and predictability. This cognitive style is linked to a desire for stability and tradition, making conservatives more likely to resist change and uphold established norms and institutions. They often prefer clear, black-and-white distinctions and may be more skeptical of new ideas or social innovations that could disrupt the social order.

Risk Perception and Threat Sensitivity

Another significant psychological difference between progressives and conservatives involves their perception of risk and sensitivity to threats.

- **Conservative Personalities**: Research has shown that conservatives generally have a heightened sensitivity to perceived threats and are more likely to prioritize security and stability. This heightened threat sensitivity can manifest in a preference for strong national defense, stricter immigration policies, and a focus on law and order. Conservatives are often more vigilant about potential dangers, whether they are social, economic, or political, and this vigilance can lead them to support policies that they believe will protect their communities and way of life.
- **Progressive Personalities**: Progressives tend to be less sensitive to perceived threats and more focused on social change and addressing systemic issues, such as inequality and injustice. While they also care about safety and security, they are more likely to view these issues through the lens of social justice and human rights. For example, progressives may support criminal justice reform or more compassionate immigration policies, believing that these

approaches are necessary to create a more equitable and just society, even if they involve some level of risk or uncertainty.

Moral Foundations and Values

The psychology of political orientation is also deeply connected to underlying moral foundations and values. According to the Moral Foundations Theory, proposed by psychologists Jonathan Haidt and his colleagues, conservatives and progressives emphasize different moral values when making decisions.

- **Conservative Moral Foundations**: Conservatives tend to prioritize values such as **loyalty, authority**, and **sanctity**. These values reflect a respect for tradition, a belief in the importance of hierarchical social structures, and a commitment to the cohesion and stability of the group or nation. Conservatives are often motivated by a sense of duty to uphold social norms and protect their community from external and internal threats. They are more likely to view social order and moral clarity as essential to the functioning of society.
- **Progressive Moral Foundations**: Progressives, in contrast, are more likely to emphasize values such as **care, fairness**, and **equality**. These

values are aligned with a concern for the well-being of others, particularly marginalized or disadvantaged groups. Progressives are motivated by a desire to reduce suffering, promote social justice, and challenge power structures that they perceive as oppressive or unfair. They tend to be more egalitarian in their outlook, seeking to level the playing field and ensure that everyone has an equal opportunity to succeed.

Social Identity and Group Dynamics

Social identity and group dynamics also play a significant role in shaping political personalities. People often align themselves with political groups that reflect their values, beliefs, and social identities, and these affiliations can reinforce their political orientation.

- **Conservative Social Identity**: Conservatives often derive a strong sense of identity from their affiliation with traditional social groups, such as religious communities, national identities, or cultural heritage. These group affiliations provide a sense of belonging and purpose, and they can be a source of pride and stability. Conservative individuals may be more likely to prioritize the interests of their in-group and to view outsiders or different social groups with suspicion or as potential threats to their way of life.

- **Progressive Social Identity**: Progressives, on the other hand, may identify more strongly with diverse and inclusive social groups, such as those advocating for civil rights, environmental justice, or global cooperation. They often see their identity as being tied to broader humanistic or cosmopolitan values, which can lead them to advocate for policies that promote inclusivity and diversity. Progressives are generally more open to forming alliances across different social groups and may be more supportive of multiculturalism and globalism.

Emotional Responses and Political Engagement

The emotional responses of individuals to political issues can also differ based on their political orientation.

- **Conservative Emotional Responses**: Conservatives are more likely to experience emotions such as fear or anger in response to perceived threats, which can drive them to support policies that they believe will protect their community or nation. These emotional responses are closely linked to the conservative emphasis on security and order, and they can lead to a strong commitment to defending traditional values and institutions.

- **Progressive Emotional Responses**: Progressives, by contrast, are often driven by emotions such as empathy and compassion, particularly when they perceive injustice or suffering. These emotions can motivate progressives to engage in activism and support policies aimed at alleviating poverty, reducing inequality, or protecting the environment. Progressives may also experience a sense of moral outrage when they perceive that the rights or dignity of individuals are being violated, which can fuel their commitment to social change.

Conclusion

The psychological differences between progressives and conservatives are complex and multifaceted, involving variations in cognitive styles, risk perception, moral foundations, social identity, and emotional responses. These differences shape not only how individuals think about political issues but also how they engage with the world around them.

Understanding these psychological underpinnings can provide valuable insights into the motivations and behaviors of people on both sides of the political spectrum, helping to explain why certain policies resonate more with one group than another and why political debates often become deeply personal and emotionally charged. Despite these differences, both progressives and conservatives contribute to the dynamic interplay of ideas that drives democratic societies, and recognizing the psychological basis of these differences can promote greater empathy and understanding across the political divide.

Economic Class Division: Understanding Socioeconomic Stratification

Defining Economic Class Division

Economic class division refers to the stratification of society based on individuals' economic status, wealth, and income. This division results in the formation of different social classes, each with distinct levels of access to resources, opportunities, and power. Economic class divisions are a fundamental aspect of nearly every society, influencing not only economic outcomes but also social, cultural, and political dynamics.

The concept of economic class is often understood in terms of a hierarchy, where individuals or groups are categorized as upper, middle, or lower class, depending on their economic standing. These classes are typically associated with varying degrees of wealth, education, occupation, and lifestyle, and they often play a crucial role in shaping an individual's life chances, social identity, and access to opportunities.

Historical Context of Economic Class Division

The division of society into different economic classes has deep historical roots, dating back to the early stages of civilization. In ancient societies, class divisions were often based on occupation, land ownership, and birthright. For example, feudal systems in medieval Europe created rigid class structures based on land ownership, with nobility, clergy, and peasants occupying distinct social positions.

The Industrial Revolution, which began in the late 18th century, significantly transformed economic class structures by creating new economic opportunities and challenges. The rise of industrial capitalism led to the emergence of a new class of wealthy industrialists and entrepreneurs, as well as a large working class employed in factories and mines. This period also saw the expansion of the middle class, composed of professionals, managers, and small business owners, who occupied a position between the wealthy elite and the working class.

Over time, the economic class structure continued to evolve, influenced by factors such as technological advancements, globalization, and changes in government policies. Today, economic class divisions are shaped by a complex interplay of factors, including income inequality, access to education and healthcare, and the availability of social safety nets.

The Three Main Economic Classes

While there are many ways to categorize economic classes, a common framework divides society into three broad classes: the upper class, the middle class, and the lower class. Each of these classes is characterized by distinct economic conditions, social status, and opportunities.

1. **Upper Class**: The upper class is composed of individuals and families who possess significant wealth, often accumulated through investments, business ownership, or inheritance. Members of the upper class typically have high incomes, substantial assets, and access to elite social networks. They often hold positions of power and influence in business, politics, and culture. The upper class enjoys a high standard of living, with access to the best education, healthcare, and other resources. This class is often associated with luxury, prestige, and exclusivity.

2. **Middle Class**: The middle class is a diverse group that includes professionals, managers, small business owners, and skilled workers. Members of the middle class typically have moderate to high incomes, stable employment, and a certain level of economic security. The middle class is often seen as the backbone of the

economy, playing a crucial role in driving consumer demand, supporting social stability, and contributing to civic life. However, the middle class can be further divided into upper-middle and lower-middle segments, with the former enjoying greater economic stability and opportunities than the latter.

3. **Lower Class**: The lower class consists of individuals and families who have limited economic resources, often characterized by low incomes, job insecurity, and limited access to education and healthcare. The lower class includes low-wage workers, the unemployed, and those living in poverty. Members of the lower class often face significant barriers to upward mobility, including lack of access to quality education, affordable housing, and job opportunities. This class is more vulnerable to economic downturns and often relies on government assistance programs for basic needs.

Economic Inequality and Class Mobility

Economic inequality, the unequal distribution of wealth and income, is a key factor in economic class division. As inequality increases, the gap between the upper, middle, and lower classes widens, leading to greater disparities in living standards, opportunities, and social outcomes. In many societies, economic inequality has been on the rise in recent decades, driven by factors such as globalization, technological change, and policy decisions that favor the wealthy.

Class mobility, or the ability to move between economic classes, is another important aspect of economic class division. In theory, a society with high class mobility would allow individuals to improve their economic standing through hard work, education, and innovation. However, in practice, class mobility is often limited by structural barriers, such as unequal access to education, discrimination, and the concentration of wealth and power among the elite.

In societies with low class mobility, individuals born into lower economic classes may find it difficult to escape poverty or achieve upward mobility, while those born into wealthier classes are more likely to maintain or even increase their economic advantage. This lack of mobility can perpetuate economic inequality and contribute to social tension and conflict.

The Social and Cultural Impacts of Economic Class Division

Economic class division has profound social and cultural implications. The class into which an individual is born or in which they find themselves can significantly influence their life experiences, values, and worldview.

- **Education**: Access to quality education is often stratified by economic class, with wealthier families able to afford private schooling, tutoring, and higher education, while lower-income families may struggle to access even basic educational resources. This disparity in educational opportunities can reinforce economic class divisions, as education is a key determinant of future income and social mobility.
- **Health**: Economic class also affects access to healthcare and overall health outcomes. Wealthier individuals typically have better access to healthcare services, healthier living conditions, and the resources to maintain a healthy lifestyle. In contrast, those in lower economic classes may face challenges such as limited access to healthcare, poor living conditions, and higher rates of chronic illness, all of which contribute to poorer health outcomes.
- **Social Identity and Status**: Economic class is a significant component of social identity, influencing how individuals perceive themselves and how they are perceived by others. Class status can affect one's social network, cultural tastes, and even political views. For example,

members of the upper class may identify with elite cultural practices and have greater influence in shaping social norms, while those in lower classes may develop subcultures that reflect their distinct experiences and challenges.

- **Political Power and Influence**: Economic class division also plays a critical role in shaping political power and influence. The wealthy often have greater access to political decision-makers and can use their resources to influence policy through campaign contributions, lobbying, and media ownership. This can lead to policies that favor the interests of the upper class, further entrenching economic inequality. Meanwhile, those in lower economic classes may have less political influence and face greater obstacles in advocating for policies that address their needs.

Responses to Economic Class Division

Addressing economic class division and the associated inequality requires a multifaceted approach, including policy interventions, social programs, and efforts to promote greater class mobility.

1. **Economic Policies**: Governments can implement policies aimed at reducing economic inequality, such as progressive taxation, minimum wage

laws, and social welfare programs. These policies can help redistribute wealth, provide support for those in need, and create opportunities for upward mobility.

2. **Education and Training**: Expanding access to quality education and vocational training is essential for promoting class mobility. By ensuring that all individuals have the opportunity to develop the skills and knowledge needed to succeed in the labor market, societies can help break the cycle of poverty and create a more equitable distribution of economic opportunities.

3. **Healthcare Access**: Ensuring that all individuals have access to affordable healthcare is crucial for reducing health disparities across economic classes. Public health initiatives, expanded healthcare coverage, and targeted interventions in underserved communities can help improve health outcomes and reduce the impact of economic inequality on health.

4. **Social Inclusion and Empowerment**: Efforts to promote social inclusion and empower marginalized communities can help address the social and cultural impacts of economic class division. This includes supporting community organizations, promoting diversity and

representation, and encouraging civic participation among all economic classes.

5. **Global Perspective**: Addressing economic class division also requires a global perspective, as economic inequality is not limited to individual countries but is a global phenomenon. International cooperation on issues such as trade, taxation, and labor rights is essential for addressing the root causes of global economic inequality and promoting more equitable development.

Conclusion

Economic class division is a deeply ingrained aspect of society that influences nearly every aspect of life, from education and health to social identity and political power. Understanding the dynamics of economic class division is essential for addressing the challenges of inequality and creating a more just and equitable society. By recognizing the complexities of economic class and implementing policies and programs that promote greater equality and opportunity, societies can work toward reducing the impact of economic class division and ensuring that all individuals have the chance to succeed.

Economic Inequality: Historical Context and Contemporary Dynamics

Introduction

Economic inequality, the unequal distribution of wealth, income, and resources, has been a defining feature of human societies for centuries. While its manifestations and drivers have evolved over time, the impact of economic inequality on social, economic, and political life remains profound. This discussion explores how economic inequality has developed historically and how it continues to occur in the modern world, highlighting key factors and consequences.

Historical Context of Economic Inequality

Economic inequality has existed since the earliest organized societies, though its forms and severity have varied across different periods and cultures.

1. **Ancient Societies**: In early agrarian and hunter-gatherer societies, economic inequality was relatively limited, as resources were often shared communally. However, with the advent of agriculture and the formation of settled communities, wealth began to accumulate in the hands of those who controlled land and resources. This led to the development of class

structures, with elites who owned land and slaves at the top, and peasants or serfs at the bottom. In ancient civilizations like Egypt, Mesopotamia, and Rome, economic inequality was stark, with wealth concentrated in the hands of a ruling class that controlled vast territories and resources.

2. **Feudalism**: During the medieval period, the feudal system further entrenched economic inequality. Land ownership was the primary determinant of wealth, and society was divided into rigid classes: the nobility, who owned the land, and the peasantry, who worked it. The feudal lords provided protection and governance in exchange for labor and tribute, creating a system where economic mobility was nearly impossible. This period also saw the rise of the church as a significant economic power, further reinforcing the hierarchical structure of society.

3. **The Industrial Revolution**: The Industrial Revolution, beginning in the late 18th century, dramatically altered the economic landscape and reshaped patterns of inequality. The transition from agrarian economies to industrialized ones created new wealth for factory owners, entrepreneurs, and financiers, while also giving rise to a growing working class. However, the benefits of industrialization were unevenly

distributed. Factory workers often faced harsh conditions, low wages, and limited rights, while the emerging capitalist class accumulated substantial wealth. This era marked the beginning of significant economic inequality in industrialized nations, with wealth increasingly concentrated among those who controlled capital and industrial production.

4. **The 20th Century and the Welfare State**: The 20th century brought significant changes to economic inequality, particularly in the West. The Great Depression, World Wars, and the rise of socialist and labor movements led to the establishment of welfare states in many countries. Progressive taxation, social security, public education, and healthcare systems were introduced to reduce economic disparities and provide a safety net for the vulnerable. As a result, the mid-20th century saw a period of relatively low economic inequality in many Western nations. However, this trend began to reverse in the late 20th century, as neoliberal economic policies, deregulation, and globalization led to a resurgence of inequality.

5. **Global Economic Inequality**: On a global scale, economic inequality has been shaped by colonialism, imperialism, and the global division

of labor. Colonial powers extracted resources and wealth from colonized regions, creating lasting economic disparities between the developed and developing worlds. Post-colonial nations often struggled with poverty, debt, and underdevelopment, while former colonial powers continued to benefit from the legacy of exploitation. Today, global inequality remains a significant challenge, with vast differences in income, wealth, and living standards between countries.

Contemporary Drivers of Economic Inequality

In the modern era, economic inequality is driven by a complex interplay of factors, many of which are interconnected and mutually reinforcing.

1. **Technological Change**: Technological advancements, particularly in automation and information technology, have transformed the global economy. While these changes have created new opportunities and industries, they have also contributed to economic inequality by disproportionately benefiting those with the skills and resources to capitalize on them. High-skilled workers and tech entrepreneurs have seen significant income growth, while low-skilled

workers face job displacement and wage stagnation. The rise of the digital economy has also led to the concentration of wealth among a small number of tech giants and their founders.

2. **Globalization**: Globalization has integrated economies around the world, increasing trade, investment, and the movement of labor. While globalization has lifted millions out of poverty in developing countries, it has also contributed to rising inequality within countries. In developed nations, globalization has led to the decline of manufacturing jobs, wage pressure on low-skilled workers, and the outsourcing of labor to cheaper markets. At the same time, it has enabled multinational corporations and investors to accumulate vast wealth, often with limited accountability to any single nation.

3. **Policy Decisions**: Government policies play a crucial role in shaping economic inequality. In recent decades, many countries have adopted neoliberal policies, including deregulation, privatization, and tax cuts for the wealthy, which have contributed to rising inequality. For example, lower taxes on capital gains and inheritance have disproportionately benefited the wealthy, while cuts to social programs have exacerbated hardships for the poor. Labor market

policies, such as the weakening of unions and the rise of precarious employment, have also contributed to wage inequality.

4. **Education and Skill Gaps**: Access to education is a key determinant of economic mobility and inequality. In many countries, there are significant disparities in educational opportunities based on socioeconomic status, race, and geography. These disparities limit the ability of individuals from disadvantaged backgrounds to acquire the skills needed for high-paying jobs. Rising education costs and student debt further exacerbate these inequalities, making it difficult for many to pursue higher education and improve their economic prospects.

5. **Wealth Accumulation and Inheritance**: Wealth inequality is often more pronounced than income inequality, as wealth tends to accumulate and concentrate over generations. Those born into wealthy families have access to resources, networks, and opportunities that facilitate further wealth accumulation. Inheritance and intergenerational transfers of wealth perpetuate economic disparities, making it difficult for those from lower economic backgrounds to achieve upward mobility. The concentration of wealth in the hands of a few also increases their political

and economic power, further entrenching inequality.

6. **Labor Market Dynamics**: Changes in the labor market, including the rise of the gig economy, temporary work, and part-time employment, have contributed to economic inequality. These forms of employment often come with lower wages, fewer benefits, and less job security, disproportionately affecting lower-income workers. The decline of unions and collective bargaining power has also weakened workers' ability to negotiate for better wages and working conditions, leading to wage stagnation and growing income inequality.

7. **Discrimination and Social Inequities**: Systemic discrimination based on race, gender, ethnicity, and other social identities continues to drive economic inequality. Minority groups often face barriers to education, employment, and wealth accumulation, resulting in persistent income and wealth gaps. Gender inequality, for example, is evident in the wage gap, underrepresentation in leadership positions, and the disproportionate burden of unpaid care work on women. These social inequities are both a cause and a consequence of economic inequality.

8. **Housing and Geographic Inequality**: Access to affordable housing and the geographic distribution of economic opportunities are significant factors in economic inequality. Urban areas with high living costs can exclude lower-income individuals, while rural areas may lack access to quality education, healthcare, and employment opportunities. This geographic inequality often exacerbates other forms of economic disparity, as those in disadvantaged areas have fewer opportunities for upward mobility.

Consequences of Economic Inequality

Economic inequality has profound implications for individuals, societies, and economies.

1. **Social Mobility**: High levels of economic inequality can impede social mobility, making it difficult for individuals to improve their economic status through education and hard work. This lack of mobility can lead to frustration, reduced motivation, and a sense of injustice among lower-income groups.
2. **Economic Growth**: While some level of inequality can incentivize innovation and hard work, excessive inequality can hinder economic

growth. It can lead to underinvestment in education and health for large segments of the population, reduce consumer demand, and create social unrest that disrupts economic activity.

3. **Health and Well-being**: Economic inequality is linked to disparities in health outcomes, with lower-income individuals experiencing higher rates of chronic illnesses, lower life expectancy, and limited access to healthcare. These health disparities not only affect individual well-being but also have broader societal costs in terms of healthcare spending and lost productivity.

4. **Political Stability and Democracy**: Significant economic disparities can undermine political stability and democratic institutions. Wealth concentration can lead to disproportionate political influence for the wealthy, resulting in policies that favor their interests over those of the broader population. This can erode trust in government, increase political polarization, and foster social unrest.

5. **Crime and Social Conflict**: High levels of inequality are associated with increased rates of crime and social conflict. Economic desperation and frustration among marginalized groups can lead to higher incidences of criminal activity and social tensions.

Addressing Economic Inequality

Addressing economic inequality requires a multifaceted approach that includes policy reforms, social interventions, and structural changes.

1. **Progressive Taxation**: Implementing progressive tax systems where higher incomes are taxed at higher rates can help redistribute wealth and reduce income disparities.
2. **Education and Training**: Investing in education and vocational training programs ensures that individuals have the skills needed to compete in a modern economy, promoting social mobility and reducing skill gaps.
3. **Social Safety Nets**: Expanding social welfare programs, including unemployment benefits, healthcare, and housing assistance, provides support to those in need and helps level the playing field.
4. **Labor Market Reforms**: Strengthening labor protections, supporting unionization, and ensuring fair wages can help reduce income inequality and improve working conditions.
5. **Wealth Redistribution**: Policies aimed at wealth redistribution, such as inheritance taxes and capital gains taxes, can prevent excessive

concentration of wealth and promote a more
equitable distribution of resources.

6. **Addressing Discrimination**: Implementing anti-
    discrimination laws and promoting diversity and
    inclusion in education, employment, and other
    sectors can help reduce economic disparities
    based on race, gender, and other social identities.

7. **Affordable Housing and Urban Planning**:
    Ensuring access to affordable housing and
    equitable urban planning can mitigate geographic
    disparities and promote economic opportunities
    across different regions.

Conclusion

Economic inequality is a complex and multifaceted
issue with deep historical roots and contemporary
drivers. Understanding its origins and mechanisms is
essential for developing effective strategies to address
it. By implementing comprehensive policies that
promote education, fair taxation, social safety nets, and
equal opportunities, societies can work towards
reducing economic disparities and fostering a more
inclusive and equitable world.

Unbridled Capitalism: A Critical Examination

Introduction

Unbridled capitalism refers to a form of capitalism where there are few or no regulations or controls placed on the market by the government. It embodies the idea that markets, when left to their own devices, will self-regulate, efficiently allocate resources, and maximize wealth and innovation. However, while unbridled capitalism can lead to rapid economic growth and technological advancements, it also has significant drawbacks. This exploration delves into the nature of unbridled capitalism, its historical roots, benefits, and the various criticisms it faces due to its social, economic, and environmental consequences.

The Core Principles of Capitalism

To understand unbridled capitalism, it's essential first to grasp the foundational principles of capitalism:

1. **Private Ownership**: Capitalism is based on the idea that individuals and corporations have the right to own and control property and businesses. This ownership extends to the means of production, such as factories, land, and capital.
2. **Market Economy**: In a capitalist system, goods and services are produced and exchanged in a

market, where supply and demand determine prices. The market is seen as the most efficient way to allocate resources.

3. **Profit Motive**: The driving force behind capitalism is the pursuit of profit. Businesses and individuals are motivated by the desire to maximize their financial gains.

4. **Competition**: Competition between businesses is believed to drive innovation, improve quality, and lower prices, ultimately benefiting consumers.

5. **Minimal Government Intervention**: Classical economic theory posits that the government's role should be limited, primarily focusing on protecting property rights, enforcing contracts, and maintaining law and order.

The Emergence of Unbridled Capitalism

Unbridled capitalism is often associated with the economic philosophy of **laissez-faire**, which advocates for minimal government interference in the market. This concept became particularly influential during the Industrial Revolution in the 18th and 19th centuries, a period characterized by rapid economic growth, industrialization, and the rise of powerful business magnates.

1. **The Industrial Revolution**: The Industrial
    Revolution marked the beginning of large-scale
    unbridled capitalism. The transition from
    agrarian economies to industrialized production
    brought about significant economic changes.
    Entrepreneurs and industrialists, often referred to
    as "robber barons" in the United States, amassed
    vast fortunes by capitalizing on the lack of
    regulations, exploiting labor, and manipulating
    markets. Figures like John D. Rockefeller and
    Andrew Carnegie became symbols of unbridled
    capitalism, accumulating wealth and power with
    little regard for workers' rights or environmental
    impacts.

2. **The Gilded Age**: The late 19th century in the
    United States, often referred to as the Gilded
    Age, is a prime example of unbridled capitalism.
    During this period, economic growth was
    unprecedented, but so was economic inequality.
    The lack of labor laws and regulations allowed
    for the exploitation of workers, including child
    labor, unsafe working conditions, and extremely
    low wages. Meanwhile, monopolies and trusts
    formed, allowing a few individuals and
    corporations to dominate entire industries,
    stifling competition and controlling prices.

3. **Neoliberalism**: The late 20th century saw a resurgence of unbridled capitalism under the guise of neoliberalism, an economic ideology that advocates for deregulation, privatization, and free markets. Leaders like Margaret Thatcher in the United Kingdom and Ronald Reagan in the United States championed policies that reduced government intervention in the economy, leading to significant deregulation of industries, reduction in social welfare programs, and tax cuts for the wealthy. This era also saw the rise of globalization, which further fueled unbridled capitalism by enabling multinational corporations to operate across borders with minimal regulation.

Benefits of Unbridled Capitalism

Proponents of unbridled capitalism argue that it has several significant advantages:

1. **Economic Growth**: Unbridled capitalism can lead to rapid economic growth. By removing barriers to entrepreneurship and innovation, it encourages investment, job creation, and technological advancement. The industrial and technological revolutions, fueled by unregulated

markets, are often cited as examples of the economic benefits of unbridled capitalism.

2. **Innovation**: The competition inherent in unbridled capitalism incentivizes businesses to innovate. Companies that fail to innovate may be driven out of the market by more innovative competitors, creating a dynamic environment that fosters technological and product development.

3. **Wealth Creation**: Unbridled capitalism has been responsible for creating immense wealth. By allowing individuals and businesses to accumulate capital and reinvest profits, it can generate wealth at unprecedented levels. This wealth, in theory, can trickle down through investment, job creation, and philanthropy.

4. **Consumer Choice**: In a capitalist economy, competition leads to a wide array of choices for consumers. Businesses must continually improve their products and services to attract customers, resulting in better quality, lower prices, and more options.

Criticisms of Unbridled Capitalism

Despite its potential benefits, unbridled capitalism has been the subject of intense criticism due to its numerous negative consequences.

1. **Economic Inequality**: One of the most significant criticisms of unbridled capitalism is that it exacerbates economic inequality. Wealth tends to concentrate in the hands of a few, leading to a widening gap between the rich and the poor. This inequality can lead to social unrest, reduced social mobility, and a sense of injustice among those left behind.

2. **Exploitation of Labor**: Without regulations, businesses may prioritize profits over the well-being of workers. This can result in poor working conditions, low wages, and the exploitation of vulnerable populations, including children. The Industrial Revolution provides numerous examples of such exploitation, where workers faced dangerous conditions, long hours, and little recourse for grievances.

3. **Environmental Degradation**: Unbridled capitalism often prioritizes short-term profits over long-term sustainability. This can lead to environmental degradation as businesses exploit natural resources without considering the environmental impact. Pollution, deforestation, and climate change are all consequences of unchecked industrial activity driven by profit motives.

4. **Market Failures**: Unregulated markets are not always efficient and can lead to market failures. Monopolies, where a single company controls an entire market, can stifle competition, leading to higher prices and reduced innovation. Additionally, the financial sector, when left unregulated, can engage in risky behavior that leads to economic crises, such as the 2008 financial collapse.

5. **Social and Moral Implications**: Unbridled capitalism can lead to a society where material wealth is valued above all else, eroding social cohesion and moral values. The pursuit of profit may overshadow considerations of social justice, equity, and the common good, leading to a society that is increasingly divided and unequal.

6. **Political Corruption and Influence**: Wealth concentration in an unbridled capitalist system can lead to disproportionate political influence for the wealthy. This can result in policies that favor the rich and powerful, further entrenching inequality and undermining democratic processes. The influence of money in politics, especially in lobbying and campaign financing, is a significant concern in many countries,

Responses to Unbridled Capitalism

In response to the negative consequences of unbridled capitalism, various strategies and systems have been proposed and implemented to mitigate its effects.

1. **Regulation and Oversight**: One of the most common responses to unbridled capitalism is the implementation of regulations that protect workers, consumers, and the environment. Labor laws, antitrust regulations, environmental protections, and financial oversight are all mechanisms designed to curb the excesses of capitalism while maintaining its benefits.

2. **Welfare State and Social Safety Nets**: To address the inequality and social disparities created by unbridled capitalism, many countries have developed welfare states and social safety nets. These include social security, healthcare, unemployment benefits, and public education, all of which help to reduce poverty and provide opportunities for social mobility.

3. **Corporate Social Responsibility (CSR)**: In recent decades, there has been a growing emphasis on corporate social responsibility, where businesses voluntarily adopt ethical practices, support social causes, and work towards sustainability. CSR is seen as a way for

businesses to balance profit-making with social good, though critics argue that it is often more about public relations than genuine commitment to change.

4. **Alternative Economic Models**: Some propose alternative economic models that challenge the tenets of unbridled capitalism. These include mixed economies, where the government plays a significant role in regulating and providing services, and social democracies, which combine a capitalist economy with strong social welfare programs. Additionally, movements such as socialism and cooperativism advocate for collective ownership and control of resources, aiming to reduce inequality and ensure that wealth is distributed more equitably.

Conclusion

Unbridled capitalism, while capable of driving significant economic growth and innovation, also carries with it severe risks and drawbacks. The lack of regulation can lead to extreme inequality, exploitation, environmental damage, and social unrest. Addressing these issues requires a balanced approach that harnesses the strengths of capitalism while mitigating its excesses through regulation, social safety nets, and ethical business practices. The challenge lies in finding the right balance between market freedom and social responsibility, ensuring that economic prosperity is inclusive and sustainable.

Corporate Manipulation of Policy and the Economy

Introduction

Corporate manipulation of policy and the economy refers to the strategies and tactics used by large corporations to influence government regulations, economic policies, and market conditions to favor their interests. This manipulation often involves lobbying, campaign contributions, regulatory capture, and other forms of influence that allow corporations to shape the rules of the game to their advantage. While businesses have a legitimate interest in advocating for favorable policies, the extent to which some corporations manipulate the system can lead to significant economic, social, and political consequences. This discussion explores the mechanisms of corporate manipulation, its historical and contemporary examples, and its impacts on society.

Mechanisms of Corporate Manipulation

Corporations employ a variety of methods to influence policy and the economy, often leveraging their financial resources, networks, and strategic positioning to achieve their goals.

1. **Lobbying**: Lobbying is one of the most direct and visible forms of corporate influence.

Corporations hire lobbyists—often former government officials or experts in specific industries—to advocate for their interests with lawmakers and regulators. Lobbyists provide policymakers with information, draft legislation, and attempt to sway opinions on issues ranging from tax policy to environmental regulations. In some cases, corporate lobbying can lead to the passage of laws that benefit specific industries or companies at the expense of the public interest. For example, the financial industry's lobbying efforts have been credited with shaping deregulation policies that contributed to the 2008 financial crisis.

2. **Campaign Contributions and Political Donations**: Corporations and their executives often make substantial contributions to political campaigns, political action committees (PACs), and super PACs. These donations can help secure access to politicians and influence their positions on key issues. While direct quid pro quo arrangements are illegal, the expectation of favorable treatment for donors is a well-recognized dynamic in politics. This influence is particularly pronounced in countries like the United States, where campaign finance laws allow for significant corporate contributions. The

Citizens United v. FEC Supreme Court decision in 2010, which allowed unlimited corporate spending in elections, has been a major factor in increasing corporate influence in politics.

3. **Regulatory Capture**: Regulatory capture occurs when regulatory agencies, which are supposed to oversee and regulate industries in the public interest, are effectively controlled or heavily influenced by the industries they are supposed to regulate. This can happen when former industry executives are appointed to key regulatory positions or when regulators become overly reliant on industry-provided information. As a result, regulations may be weakened, enforcement may be lax, and policies may be tailored to benefit corporations rather than protect consumers or the environment. An example of regulatory capture is the relationship between the pharmaceutical industry and the U.S. Food and Drug Administration (FDA), where concerns have been raised about the influence of drug companies on the approval process for new medications.

4. **Astroturfing and Public Relations**: Corporations often engage in "astroturfing," a tactic where they create or fund fake grassroots organizations that appear to represent public

opinion but actually serve corporate interests. These organizations can lobby for or against specific policies, create the illusion of widespread public support or opposition, and sway public discourse. In addition to astroturfing, corporations use public relations campaigns to shape public perception and influence policy debates. By controlling the narrative through media campaigns, advertising, and sponsored content, corporations can build support for their positions on key issues. For example, the tobacco industry famously used astroturf groups and PR campaigns to cast doubt on the health risks of smoking for decades.

5. **Think Tanks and Research Funding**: Corporations often fund think tanks, research institutions, and academic studies to produce reports and analyses that support their positions. These organizations can provide policymakers and the public with seemingly independent evidence and expert opinions, which may actually be biased by the interests of their corporate sponsors. This tactic can be particularly effective in shaping long-term policy debates and framing issues in ways that benefit corporate interests. For instance, fossil fuel companies have funded research that downplays the impact of

climate change or advocates for minimal
regulatory intervention, influencing energy
policies in their favor.

6. **Legal Strategies and Litigation**: Corporations
frequently use the legal system to influence
policy and protect their interests. They may
challenge regulations in court, sue governments
for damages under international trade
agreements, or use strategic litigation to delay or
block unfavorable policies. The threat of costly
legal battles can also deter governments from
pursuing certain regulations or enforcing existing
laws, giving corporations leverage over public
policy. Additionally, corporations may lobby for
legal reforms that limit liability, reduce
regulatory burdens, or create more favorable
business environments. An example is the use of
investor-state dispute settlement (ISDS)
mechanisms in trade agreements, which allow
corporations to sue governments for enacting
policies that allegedly harm their profits.

Historical and Contemporary Examples

Throughout history, corporations have played a
significant role in shaping economic and political
landscapes. Some notable examples include:

1. **The Gilded Age and the Rise of Monopolies**: In the late 19th and early 20th centuries, the United States experienced a period of rapid industrialization known as the Gilded Age. During this time, powerful corporations and monopolies, such as Standard Oil and U.S. Steel, wielded enormous influence over the economy and government. These corporations used their wealth and connections to lobby for favorable policies, suppress competition, and manipulate markets. The public backlash against these practices eventually led to the implementation of antitrust laws, such as the Sherman Antitrust Act of 1890, designed to break up monopolies and prevent corporate overreach.

2. **The Military-Industrial Complex**: The term "military-industrial complex" was popularized by President Dwight D. Eisenhower in his 1961 farewell address, warning of the growing influence of defense contractors and the military establishment on U.S. policy. The defense industry has long been a major player in U.S. politics, using lobbying, campaign contributions, and revolving-door employment practices to secure lucrative government contracts and influence national security policies. This relationship has led to concerns about excessive

military spending, the perpetuation of conflicts, and the prioritization of corporate profits over national interests.

3. **Big Tech and Data Privacy**: In the 21st century, technology companies like Facebook, Google, and Amazon have become some of the most powerful entities in the global economy. These companies have used their influence to shape data privacy laws, antitrust regulations, and other policies that affect their business models. For example, Facebook has been accused of lobbying against stricter privacy regulations in the European Union and the United States, while Google has faced antitrust investigations and fines for using its market dominance to stifle competition. The vast amounts of data these companies control, combined with their lobbying power, have raised concerns about their influence over democratic processes and individual freedoms.

4. **Pharmaceutical Industry and Drug Pricing**: The pharmaceutical industry is one of the most prominent examples of corporate manipulation of policy, particularly in the area of drug pricing. Pharmaceutical companies have used lobbying, campaign contributions, and regulatory capture to influence policies that allow them to set high

prices for medications, extend patents, and delay the entry of generic drugs into the market. The result is often exorbitant prices for essential medications, placing a significant burden on consumers and healthcare systems. The opioid crisis in the United States, fueled by aggressive marketing and lobbying by pharmaceutical companies, is a stark example of the consequences of corporate influence on public health policy.

Impacts on Society

Corporate manipulation of policy and the economy has far-reaching consequences that extend beyond the economic sphere, affecting social equity, democratic governance, and environmental sustainability.

1. **Economic Inequality**: One of the most significant impacts of corporate manipulation is the exacerbation of economic inequality. When corporations successfully lobby for tax cuts, deregulation, and other policies that favor their interests, the benefits often accrue to wealthy shareholders and executives, while workers and consumers bear the costs. This dynamic contributes to the growing wealth gap between

the rich and the poor, undermining social cohesion and economic mobility.

2. **Erosion of Democracy**: Corporate influence in politics can undermine democratic processes by distorting policy outcomes in favor of special interests. When corporations use their financial power to shape legislation, they often do so at the expense of the broader public interest, leading to policies that reflect the preferences of a wealthy minority rather than the will of the majority. This erosion of democratic accountability can lead to public disillusionment with political institutions and a decline in trust in government.

3. **Environmental Degradation**: Corporate manipulation of environmental policy is a major contributor to environmental degradation and climate change. Industries that profit from the extraction and use of natural resources, such as fossil fuels, agriculture, and mining, often lobby against environmental regulations and climate action. The result is weaker environmental protections, continued reliance on unsustainable practices, and a lack of progress in addressing global environmental challenges. The influence of the fossil fuel industry on climate policy is a prime example of how corporate interests can hinder efforts to combat climate change.

4. **Public Health Risks**: When corporations prioritize profits over public health, the consequences can be severe. For example, the tobacco industry's decades-long campaign to downplay the dangers of smoking led to millions of preventable deaths. Similarly, the pharmaceutical industry's influence on drug pricing and marketing has contributed to the opioid crisis, rising healthcare costs, and limited access to essential medications. Corporate manipulation of food and beverage regulations has also been linked to the global rise in obesity and related health issues.

5. **Market Distortions and Inefficiencies**: Corporate manipulation can lead to market distortions that undermine competition and efficiency. When corporations use their influence to secure monopolies, subsidies, or favorable regulations, they can stifle innovation, reduce consumer choice, and create barriers to entry for smaller competitors. These market distortions can result in higher prices, lower quality products, and a less dynamic economy.

Addressing Corporate Manipulation

Addressing the issue of corporate manipulation requires a multifaceted approach that includes regulatory reforms, transparency measures, and efforts to strengthen democratic institutions.

1. **Campaign Finance Reform**: Reforming campaign finance laws to limit corporate contributions and increase transparency is crucial to reducing the influence of money in politics. Measures such as public financing of campaigns, stricter limits on donations, and disclosure requirements can help level the playing field and ensure that elected officials are accountable to their constituents rather than special interests.

2. **Strengthening Regulatory Agencies**: Ensuring that regulatory agencies are independent, well-funded, and free from industry influence is essential to preventing regulatory capture. This includes implementing strict conflict-of-interest rules, increasing oversight of revolving-door practices, and empowering regulators to enforce laws effectively.

3. **Promoting Transparency and Accountability**: Increasing transparency around lobbying activities, political donations, and corporate influence on policymaking can help hold corporations and politicians accountable. This includes requiring the disclosure of lobbying expenditures, political donations, and funding sources for think tanks and research institutions.

4. **Empowering Civil Society and Advocacy Groups**: Civil society organizations, consumer advocacy groups, and grassroots movements play a critical role in counterbalancing corporate influence. Supporting these groups through funding, legal protections, and access to information can help amplify the voices of ordinary citizens and promote policies that reflect the public interest.

5. **International Cooperation and Regulation**: Given the global nature of many corporations, international cooperation is necessary to address cross-border issues such as tax avoidance, environmental protection, and labor rights. Developing global standards and regulatory frameworks can help ensure that corporations operate responsibly and are held accountable for their actions, regardless of where they are based.

Conclusion

Corporate manipulation of policy and the economy poses significant challenges to social equity, democratic governance, and environmental sustainability. While businesses have a legitimate role in advocating for their interests, the extent of corporate influence in shaping policy often leads to outcomes that favor the few at the expense of the many. Addressing these issues requires a concerted effort to reform campaign finance, strengthen regulatory agencies, promote transparency, and empower civil society. By doing so, societies can work towards creating a more balanced and equitable system where economic prosperity is shared, democratic processes are protected, and corporate power is held in check.

Social Democracy: A Distinct Approach

Introduction

Social democracy is a political and economic philosophy that seeks to balance individual liberty, social justice, and economic efficiency. It advocates for a mixed economy, combining elements of both capitalism and socialism to create a system that promotes both economic growth and social welfare. However, social democracy is often misunderstood and conflated with capitalism, socialism, or even communism. This exploration clarifies why social democracy stands apart from these ideologies and offers a distinct approach to governance and economic organization.

Defining Social Democracy

Social democracy is characterized by the following core principles:

1. **Mixed Economy**: Social democracy supports a mixed economy, where both private enterprise and public sector involvement coexist. It recognizes the efficiency of markets in producing goods and services but also acknowledges the need for government intervention to correct market failures and ensure social welfare.

2. **Welfare State**: A key feature of social democracy is the welfare state, which provides social safety nets such as healthcare, education, unemployment benefits, and pensions. These programs aim to reduce poverty, inequality, and social exclusion, ensuring that all citizens have access to basic needs and opportunities.

3. **Regulation of Markets**: Social democracies advocate for the regulation of markets to prevent abuses, ensure fair competition, and protect consumers, workers, and the environment. This includes labor laws, environmental regulations, antitrust policies, and financial oversight.

4. **Democratic Governance**: Social democracy emphasizes the importance of democratic governance, with strong institutions, the rule of law, and respect for human rights. It supports political pluralism, civil liberties, and the active participation of citizens in decision-making processes.

Why Social Democracy Is Not Capitalism

While social democracy incorporates elements of capitalism, it is distinct from pure capitalism in several key ways:

1. **Role of the State**: In capitalism, the role of the state is minimal, primarily focusing on protecting property rights, enforcing contracts, and maintaining law and order. Social democracy, however, assigns a much more active role to the state in regulating markets, providing public services, and redistributing wealth. The state is seen as a necessary actor in ensuring that the benefits of economic growth are shared broadly across society.

2. **Focus on Social Justice**: Capitalism prioritizes individual freedom and market efficiency, often leading to significant economic inequalities. In contrast, social democracy places a strong emphasis on social justice and reducing inequality through progressive taxation, social welfare programs, and public investment in education and healthcare. This focus on equity distinguishes social democracy from capitalism's more laissez-faire approach.

3. **Market Regulation**: While capitalism relies on the market's "invisible hand" to allocate resources and determine outcomes, social democracy actively intervenes in markets to correct inefficiencies and protect the public interest. This includes enforcing labor standards, regulating financial markets, and implementing policies that

address externalities such as pollution. The regulatory framework in social democracy is designed to balance the benefits of a market economy with the need to protect society from its excesses.

4. **Public Ownership and Social Services**: Unlike capitalism, where private ownership is the dominant model, social democracy supports public ownership of key industries and services, especially those that are essential for the public good, such as utilities, transportation, and healthcare. These services are provided by the state or heavily regulated to ensure universal access and prevent exploitation.

Why Social Democracy Is Not Socialism

Social democracy shares some similarities with socialism, particularly in its focus on social welfare and reducing inequality, but it remains distinct in several important aspects:

1. **Private Property and Markets**: Unlike socialism, which advocates for collective or state ownership of the means of production, social democracy allows for private ownership of businesses and property. Social democrats believe that markets, when properly regulated,

can be an efficient way to organize economic activity and generate wealth. They do not seek to abolish capitalism but rather to reform and humanize it through government intervention.

2. **Evolutionary, Not Revolutionary**: Social democracy is committed to achieving its goals through democratic means rather than revolution. While socialism often involves a radical transformation of society, including the overthrow of capitalism, social democracy works within the existing political and economic systems to gradually implement reforms. This evolutionary approach emphasizes pragmatism and consensus-building rather than class struggle or revolutionary change.

3. **Pluralism and Democracy**: Social democracies are committed to political pluralism and democracy, whereas traditional socialism, particularly in its Marxist-Leninist form, has often led to authoritarian regimes. Social democracy values individual freedoms, civil liberties, and the rule of law, and it seeks to balance these with social and economic rights. It rejects the idea of a one-party state or centralized control over all aspects of life.

4. **Mixed Economy vs. Planned Economy**: Socialism typically advocates for a centrally

planned economy, where the state controls all or most economic activity. Social democracy, on the other hand, supports a mixed economy where both the public and private sectors play significant roles. The state intervenes to regulate markets and provide essential services, but it does not seek to replace the market with a fully planned economy. The goal is to combine the efficiency of markets with the equity of a welfare state.

Why Social Democracy Is Not Communism

Communism represents a far more radical ideology compared to both socialism and social democracy. It envisions a classless, stateless society where all property is communally owned, and there is no need for money, markets, or a government as we know it. Social democracy, by contrast, is fundamentally different in its objectives and methods:

1. **Acceptance of Capitalism**: Communism seeks to abolish capitalism entirely, replacing it with a system of communal ownership and planned production. Social democracy, however, accepts the existence of capitalism and works to reform it. It does not aim to eliminate private property or

markets but to ensure that they operate in a way that benefits society as a whole.

2. **Democratic Institutions**: Communism, as practiced historically, often resulted in authoritarian regimes that suppressed political freedoms and individual rights in the name of building a classless society. Social democracy, in stark contrast, is committed to maintaining and strengthening democratic institutions. It views democracy not just as a means to an end but as a fundamental principle that must be upheld alongside economic and social reforms.

3. **Gradual Reform vs. Revolutionary Change**: Communism advocates for a revolutionary overthrow of the existing capitalist system, leading to the establishment of a new social order. Social democracy, however, seeks to achieve its goals through gradual, democratic reforms within the framework of a capitalist society. It relies on the existing political system to enact changes, rather than seeking to dismantle it.

4. **Class Relations**: While communism focuses on the abolition of all class distinctions, social democracy acknowledges the existence of different social classes but seeks to mitigate the inequalities between them through redistributive

policies. Social democracy does not aim to create a classless society but rather to ensure that all classes have access to opportunities and a decent standard of living.

Conclusion

Social democracy is a distinct political and economic philosophy that blends elements of capitalism and socialism while maintaining a commitment to democratic governance. It differs from capitalism by advocating for a more active role of the state in regulating markets and providing social services, and from socialism by supporting private property and markets within a mixed economy. Unlike communism, social democracy does not seek to abolish capitalism or create a classless society but rather to reform capitalism to make it more equitable and humane. By focusing on social justice, economic efficiency, and democratic principles, social democracy offers a unique approach to addressing the challenges of modern society.

The Historical 1%: Wealth and Power Through the Ages

Introduction

The term "the 1%" is widely recognized today as a reference to the small percentage of people who control a disproportionate share of wealth and power in modern societies. However, the concept of a privileged elite has deep historical roots. Throughout history, various civilizations have witnessed the concentration of wealth and power in the hands of a small elite, often comprising royalty, aristocrats, merchants, or industrialists. This exploration delves into the historical context of the 1%, examining how wealth and power have been accumulated, maintained, and challenged across different eras and societies.

The Ancient World: Dynasties and Empires

In ancient civilizations, such as those in Mesopotamia, Egypt, and China, wealth and power were typically concentrated in the hands of ruling dynasties and their closest allies. These societies were often structured as hierarchies, with a monarch or emperor at the top, supported by a class of nobles, priests, and military leaders.

1. **Egyptian Pharaohs**: In ancient Egypt, the pharaoh was considered both a political and religious leader, believed to be a god in human form. The pharaohs controlled vast wealth, which was derived from the fertile lands along the Nile River, extensive trade networks, and the labor of peasants. The construction of monumental structures, such as the pyramids, was a testament to the power and wealth concentrated in the hands of the ruling elite. The priestly class, which managed the temples and religious rites, also held significant influence, further entrenching the social and economic hierarchy.

2. **Roman Patricians and Senators**: The Roman Republic and later the Roman Empire were characterized by a sharp divide between the elite and the common people. The patricians, who were members of Rome's noble families, and the senators, who held political power, were among the wealthiest citizens. They owned vast estates, controlled significant economic resources, and held considerable influence over the government. Wealth in Rome was often derived from land ownership, trade, and the spoils of war. The concentration of wealth and power in the hands of the elite led to social tensions, including conflicts between the patricians and the plebeians

(commoners) and eventually contributed to the fall of the Republic.

3. **Chinese Emperors and Landlords**: In ancient China, the emperor was the supreme ruler, considered the "Son of Heaven," with a mandate to govern. Beneath the emperor was a complex bureaucracy composed of scholar-officials who were selected through a rigorous examination system. The wealthy landowning class, which included nobles and landlords, held significant power, often controlling large agricultural estates and exerting influence over local governance. The concentration of land in the hands of a few led to recurring issues of landlessness and poverty among peasants, contributing to periodic uprisings and social unrest.

The Middle Ages: Feudalism and the Aristocracy

The medieval period in Europe was dominated by the feudal system, a hierarchical structure where power and wealth were concentrated in the hands of the nobility and the church.

1. **Feudal Lords**: In feudal Europe, kings and queens granted land (fiefs) to nobles in exchange for military service and loyalty. These nobles, or lords, were the dominant landowners and wielded

significant economic and political power within their territories. Peasants and serfs, who made up the majority of the population, worked the land and paid tribute to their lords, reinforcing the wealth and power of the aristocracy. The feudal system was highly stratified, with little social mobility, ensuring that wealth and power remained concentrated within noble families over generations.

2. **The Catholic Church**: During the Middle Ages, the Catholic Church was one of the most powerful institutions in Europe. The Church owned vast amounts of land, collected tithes from the populace, and played a central role in the social, political, and economic life of the time. The clergy, particularly high-ranking officials such as bishops and cardinals, often came from noble families and enjoyed privileges similar to those of the secular aristocracy. The Church's influence extended beyond spiritual matters, as it often intervened in political affairs and wielded significant economic power.

3. **Medieval Merchants**: While the nobility and clergy were the primary holders of wealth and power during the Middle Ages, the rise of towns and trade in the later medieval period saw the emergence of a wealthy merchant class. These

merchants, who engaged in long-distance trade, banking, and finance, began to accumulate wealth that rivaled that of the traditional aristocracy. The rise of the merchant class laid the groundwork for the economic and social changes that would eventually lead to the decline of feudalism and the emergence of early capitalist societies.

The Renaissance and the Early Modern Period: Capitalism and Colonialism

The Renaissance and the early modern period marked significant shifts in the concentration of wealth and power, driven by the rise of capitalism, exploration, and colonialism.

1. **Renaissance Italy and the Medici Family**: The Renaissance in Italy saw the rise of powerful merchant families, such as the Medici in Florence, who amassed great wealth through banking and trade. The Medici used their wealth to influence politics, sponsor art and culture, and consolidate their power within the city-state. Their patronage of artists like Michelangelo and Leonardo da Vinci made them key figures in the cultural rebirth of Europe. The Medici family exemplifies how economic power could be

translated into political influence and cultural dominance during this period.

2. **The Age of Exploration and Colonial Empires**: The 15th and 16th centuries saw European powers, such as Spain, Portugal, the Netherlands, and England, embark on a period of exploration and colonization. The wealth generated from the exploitation of colonies, particularly through the extraction of resources like gold, silver, and spices, and the establishment of lucrative trade routes, led to the emergence of powerful colonial empires. This wealth was concentrated in the hands of monarchs, aristocrats, and wealthy merchants, who financed and profited from these ventures. The transatlantic slave trade, in particular, played a central role in the accumulation of wealth by the European elite, with devastating consequences for the enslaved populations.

3. **The Rise of Capitalist Elites**: The early modern period also saw the rise of capitalist elites, particularly in the burgeoning commercial centers of Europe. The development of joint-stock companies, such as the Dutch East India Company and the British East India Company, allowed investors to pool capital and share in the profits of global trade. These companies wielded

enormous economic and political power, often acting as quasi-sovereign entities in their colonial territories. The wealth generated by these enterprises contributed to the growth of a new capitalist class, which would eventually challenge the traditional aristocracy for dominance.

The Industrial Revolution: The Bourgeoisie and the Proletariat

The Industrial Revolution, which began in the late 18th century, brought about profound economic and social changes, leading to the emergence of new classes and the reconfiguration of wealth and power.

1. **The Industrial Bourgeoisie**: The Industrial Revolution gave rise to a new class of wealthy industrialists and entrepreneurs, known as the bourgeoisie. These individuals owned and controlled the means of production, such as factories, mines, and railroads, and amassed vast fortunes through the exploitation of labor and the expansion of industrial capitalism. The concentration of wealth in the hands of the bourgeoisie led to significant social and economic disparities, as the working class, or proletariat, toiled under harsh conditions for meager wages.

2. **Robber Barons and Gilded Age Tycoons**: In the late 19th and early 20th centuries, the United States experienced a period of rapid industrialization and economic growth known as the Gilded Age. During this time, a small group of industrial magnates, often referred to as "robber barons," accumulated enormous wealth and power. Figures such as John D. Rockefeller (oil), Andrew Carnegie (steel), and J.P. Morgan (finance) became synonymous with the excesses of unbridled capitalism. These tycoons wielded significant influence over government policies, often through corrupt practices such as bribery and monopolistic practices. The vast inequality between the wealthy elite and the working masses during this period led to social unrest and the rise of labor movements.

3. **The Advent of Welfare States and Redistribution**: The social and economic inequalities of the Industrial Revolution and the Gilded Age eventually led to demands for reform. In the 20th century, many Western countries adopted welfare state policies, which aimed to redistribute wealth and reduce inequality through progressive taxation, social security systems, and public services. These reforms were often driven by the rise of social

democratic movements, which sought to balance the benefits of capitalism with social justice. While these measures helped to mitigate some of the worst excesses of economic inequality, they did not entirely eliminate the concentration of wealth and power in the hands of the elite.

Conclusion

Throughout history, the concentration of wealth and power in the hands of a small elite—the historical 1%—has been a consistent feature of human societies. From ancient dynasties and feudal lords to industrial magnates and modern-day billionaires, the 1% has played a pivotal role in shaping economic, social, and political landscapes. However, the concentration of wealth and power has also been a source of social tension, leading to conflicts, revolutions, and demands for reform. Understanding the historical context of the 1% highlights into the ongoing challenges of inequality and the dynamics of power in contemporary society.

The Current 1%: Wealth, Power, and Influence in the 21st Century

Introduction

The term "the 1%" has become a powerful symbol in contemporary discourse, representing the small group of individuals and families who control a disproportionate share of wealth and influence in today's global economy. This modern 1% is often characterized by vast financial resources, political clout, and a significant impact on global economic trends and policies. The wealth gap between the 1% and the rest of society has become a focal point of debates about inequality, social justice, and the future of capitalism. This exploration delves into the nature of the current 1%, examining their sources of wealth, the implications of their power, and the societal consequences of such concentrated economic dominance.

The Composition of the 1%

The contemporary 1% is a diverse group, consisting of individuals from various sectors of the economy. However, several key characteristics and sources of wealth define this elite group.

1. **Tech Titans**: A significant portion of the current 1% derives its wealth from the technology sector.

Founders and executives of companies like Amazon, Apple, Google, Facebook, and Microsoft—such as Jeff Bezos, Elon Musk, Bill Gates, and Mark Zuckerberg—are among the wealthiest individuals in the world. Their wealth is often tied to the stock performance of their companies, leading to fluctuations in their net worth based on market trends. The dominance of tech giants in the global economy has not only made their founders extraordinarily wealthy but has also reshaped industries, labor markets, and even political dynamics.

2. **Financial Moguls**: Another major component of the 1% comes from the financial sector. Hedge fund managers, private equity investors, and investment bankers have accumulated vast fortunes by managing large pools of capital and profiting from financial markets. Figures like Warren Buffett, known as the "Oracle of Omaha," and major hedge fund managers like Ray Dalio and Ken Griffin are emblematic of this group. The financialization of the economy, characterized by the growing importance of financial markets and instruments, has been a significant driver of wealth accumulation for these individuals.

3. **Inherited Wealth**: While many members of the current 1% are self-made, a substantial number have inherited their wealth. Families like the Waltons (heirs to the Walmart fortune) and the Kochs (industrialists with interests in energy, manufacturing, and chemicals) exemplify how wealth can be passed down through generations. Inherited wealth often comes with established political and social networks, further entrenching the power and influence of these families. The ability to preserve and grow wealth across generations has contributed to the persistence of economic inequality.

4. **Globalization and Multinational Corporations**: The rise of globalization has also played a crucial role in the formation of the current 1%. The owners and executives of multinational corporations, which operate across borders and have access to vast markets, have seen their wealth soar. These corporations benefit from economies of scale, access to cheap labor and resources, and the ability to influence global trade and tax policies. As a result, the wealth of the 1% is increasingly global in nature, with individuals holding assets and interests in multiple countries,

The Power and Influence of the 1%

The wealth of the 1% is not just a matter of personal financial security; it translates into significant power and influence over political, economic, and social systems.

1. **Political Influence**: The 1% wields considerable influence over political processes, often through campaign contributions, lobbying, and the funding of think tanks and advocacy groups. In the United States, for example, the Supreme Court's 2010 Citizens United decision allowed for unlimited corporate and individual spending on political campaigns, amplifying the voice of wealthy donors. This has led to concerns that the political system is increasingly responsive to the interests of the wealthy rather than the broader population. The ability of the 1% to shape policy on issues ranging from taxation to regulation and trade has profound implications for economic inequality and social mobility.

2. **Control Over Media and Information**: Many members of the 1% also exert significant influence over media outlets and the flow of information. Ownership of major media companies, such as Jeff Bezos's ownership of The Washington Post, gives these individuals the

power to shape public discourse and influence public opinion. The consolidation of media ownership among a small group of wealthy individuals and corporations raises concerns about the diversity of perspectives and the role of the media in a democratic society.

3. **Impact on Global Economy**: The financial decisions and investment strategies of the 1% can have far-reaching effects on the global economy. The movement of capital by wealthy investors can influence stock markets, real estate prices, and currency values. Additionally, the concentration of wealth in the hands of a few can lead to economic instability, as the spending and investment patterns of the 1% differ significantly from those of the broader population. This can result in skewed economic growth, with benefits accruing disproportionately to the top of the income distribution.

4. **Philanthropy and Social Impact**: Many members of the 1% engage in philanthropy, donating large sums to causes such as education, health, and the arts. The Bill and Melinda Gates Foundation, for example, has become one of the most influential philanthropic organizations in the world, funding initiatives to combat diseases, improve education, and address poverty. While

philanthropy can have positive social impacts, it also raises questions about the influence of wealthy individuals over public policy and priorities. Critics argue that philanthropy can undermine democratic accountability, as decisions about resource allocation are made by a few individuals rather than through democratic processes.

The Consequences of Wealth Concentration

The concentration of wealth in the hands of the 1% has significant social, economic, and political consequences.

1. **Economic Inequality**: The growing wealth gap between the 1% and the rest of society has become a central issue in discussions about economic inequality. In many countries, the share of income and wealth held by the top 1% has increased dramatically over the past few decades, while wages for the middle and working classes have stagnated. This has led to growing concerns about social mobility, as the ability to move up the economic ladder becomes increasingly difficult in the face of entrenched wealth and privilege.

2. **Social and Political Polarization**: Economic inequality has been linked to increased social and political polarization. As the gap between the rich and the poor widens, so too does the divide between different segments of society. This can lead to social unrest, as those who feel left behind become increasingly disillusioned with the political and economic system. The rise of populist movements in many parts of the world can be seen as a reaction to the concentration of wealth and power in the hands of a few.

3. **Challenges to Democracy**: The influence of the 1% over political processes poses a challenge to democratic governance. When political power is concentrated in the hands of a wealthy elite, it can undermine the principles of equality and representation that are central to democracy. The perception that the political system is rigged in favor of the wealthy can erode trust in institutions and lead to political apathy or radicalization among the broader population.

4. **Global Implications**: The influence of the 1% extends beyond national borders, with significant implications for global governance and economic stability. The ability of multinational corporations and wealthy individuals to evade taxes, influence trade agreements, and shape

global policies has raised concerns about the erosion of national sovereignty and the ability of governments to address global challenges such as climate change, poverty, and inequality.

Conclusion

The current 1% represents a powerful and influential group that plays a central role in shaping the global economy, politics, and society. While their wealth and influence have enabled significant advancements and contributions, such as in technology and philanthropy, they also pose challenges related to economic inequality, democratic governance, and social cohesion. Understanding the dynamics of the 1% is crucial for addressing the broader issues of inequality and ensuring that the benefits of economic growth are more equitably shared across society. The debate over the role of the 1% in today's world will likely continue to shape discussions about the future of capitalism, democracy, and social justice.

Trickle-Down Economics vs. Trickle-Up Economics: A Contrast

Introduction

Trickle-down economics and trickle-up economics represent two fundamentally different approaches to economic policy and wealth distribution. These theories offer contrasting views on how to stimulate economic growth, create jobs, and reduce poverty. While trickle-down economics advocates for policies that benefit the wealthy and large corporations with the expectation that their prosperity will eventually benefit the broader economy, trickle-up economics focuses on empowering lower-income individuals and workers, believing that their increased spending will drive economic growth. Below, these two approaches are contrasted in terms of their principles, policy implications, and the criticisms they face.

Trickle-Down Economics

Principles:

Trickle-down economics is based on the belief that economic growth is most effectively stimulated by benefiting the wealthy, particularly through policies that reduce taxes and regulations on businesses, investors, and high-income individuals. Proponents argue that by creating a favorable environment for the wealthy to invest and spend, the benefits will eventually "trickle down" to the rest of society, leading to job creation, higher wages, and overall economic prosperity.

Policy Implications:

1. **Tax Cuts for the Wealthy and Corporations**: A key tenet of trickle-down economics is the reduction of taxes on the wealthy and corporations. The idea is that by lowering tax burdens, these groups will have more capital to invest in businesses, which in turn will lead to job creation, increased production, and economic growth.

2. **Deregulation**: Trickle-down economics often calls for reducing government regulations on businesses. The rationale is that fewer regulations lower the cost of doing business, allowing companies to expand, innovate, and hire more workers.

3. **Incentives for Investment**: Policies that provide incentives for investment, such as capital gains tax cuts or favorable treatment of dividends, are also central to trickle-down economics. These incentives are intended to encourage the wealthy to invest in new ventures, which are expected to lead to broader economic benefits.

Criticisms:

1. **Income Inequality**: One of the primary criticisms of trickle-down economics is that it exacerbates income inequality. Critics argue that the benefits of tax cuts and deregulation are disproportionately enjoyed by the wealthy, with little evidence that the wealth "trickles down" to lower-income individuals. This can lead to a concentration of wealth and power in the hands of a few, while the majority of people see little improvement in their economic circumstances.

2. **Limited Impact on Job Creation**: There is also skepticism about the effectiveness of trickle-down economics in creating jobs. Critics point out that companies may use tax savings for stock buybacks, dividend payments, or executive bonuses rather than investing in new jobs or higher wages for workers.

3. **Budget Deficits**: Tax cuts for the wealthy can lead to significant budget deficits, especially if they are not accompanied by corresponding cuts in government spending. This can result in reduced funding for social programs and public services, which disproportionately affects lower-income individuals.

Trickle-Up Economics

Principles:

Trickle-up economics is based on the idea that economic growth is best stimulated by empowering the lower and middle classes. The theory posits that when working-class and lower-income individuals have more disposable income, they will spend it on goods and services, thereby driving demand, boosting production, and creating jobs. This approach emphasizes the importance of a strong consumer base as the foundation of a healthy economy.

Policy Implications:

1. **Raising Wages**: A central aspect of trickle-up economics is increasing wages for lower-income workers. This can be achieved through policies such as raising the minimum wage, supporting labor unions, and implementing living wage laws. Higher wages mean more disposable income for workers, leading to increased consumer spending and economic growth.
2. **Progressive Taxation**: Trickle-up economics advocates for a progressive tax system where the wealthy pay a higher percentage of their income in taxes. The revenue generated from progressive taxation can be used to fund social programs and

public services, which benefit lower-income individuals and stimulate demand in the economy.

3. **Social Safety Nets and Public Investment**: Trickle-up economics supports robust social safety nets, including unemployment benefits, healthcare, and education. These programs not only provide a safety net for those in need but also ensure that more people have the resources and stability to participate in the economy. Public investment in infrastructure, education, and healthcare is also seen as crucial for long-term economic growth.

4. **Support for Small Businesses**: Trickle-up economics often emphasizes the importance of supporting small businesses, which are seen as engines of job creation and innovation. Policies that provide access to capital, reduce barriers to entry, and offer tax incentives for small businesses are viewed as essential for fostering a more equitable and dynamic economy.

Criticisms:

1. **Short-Term Focus**: Critics of trickle-up economics argue that it may prioritize short-term consumption over long-term investment. While increased consumer spending can boost the

economy in the short term, there are concerns that without sufficient investment in technology, infrastructure, and innovation, long-term economic growth may be hindered.

2. **Potential Inflation**: Some economists worry that policies aimed at increasing wages and expanding social programs could lead to inflation. If demand outstrips supply, prices may rise, potentially offsetting the benefits of higher wages and increased spending power for workers.

3. **Sustainability of Social Programs**: Critics also question the sustainability of extensive social programs, arguing that they require high levels of government spending and taxation, which could stifle economic growth or lead to unsustainable budget deficits.

Conclusion

Trickle-down and trickle-up economics represent opposing approaches to stimulating economic growth and addressing inequality. Trickle-down economics focuses on benefiting the wealthy with the expectation that their prosperity will eventually benefit everyone, while trickle-up economics prioritizes empowering lower-income individuals to drive demand and economic growth. Both approaches have their merits and drawbacks, and the debate between these theories continues to shape economic policy and discourse worldwide.

Wealth Redistribution: Historical Context and Contemporary Options

Introduction

Wealth redistribution has been a topic of debate and action throughout history, shaping societies and economies in significant ways. The concept involves transferring wealth from the richer segments of society to poorer ones to reduce economic inequality and create a more equitable distribution of resources. Various methods have been employed historically, ranging from land reforms to progressive taxation and welfare programs. Today, wealth redistribution continues to be a central issue, particularly in the context of growing income inequality, technological changes, and global economic shifts. This exploration provides an overview of historical approaches to wealth redistribution and examines contemporary options available to address economic inequality.

Historical Approaches to Wealth Redistribution

1. Land Reforms:

One of the earliest and most significant forms of wealth redistribution in history has been land reform. In agrarian societies, land was the primary source of wealth, and its distribution was often highly unequal, concentrated in the hands of a few landowners or elites.

- **Ancient Rome**: The Roman Republic saw several attempts at land reform, most notably the efforts of the Gracchi brothers in the 2nd century BCE. Tiberius and Gaius Gracchus proposed redistributing public land (ager publicus) held by wealthy patricians to landless citizens. Although their reforms were met with resistance and ultimately led to their deaths, the Gracchi brothers' efforts highlighted the deep social and economic inequalities of the time and the potential for wealth redistribution to address them.

- **Post-Revolutionary Land Reforms**: In the wake of revolutions, land reforms were often a critical component of broader social and economic changes. The French Revolution, for example, led to the redistribution of land owned by the Church and the aristocracy to the peasantry. Similarly, the Russian Revolution of 1917 resulted in the seizure of large estates and their redistribution among the rural population.

- **20th Century Land Reforms**: In the 20th century, land reforms were implemented in several countries as part of decolonization and socialist movements. In countries like China and

Vietnam, land reforms were central to the communist agenda, with land being taken from landlords and redistributed to peasants. In India, post-independence land reforms aimed to reduce the power of zamindars (landlords) and redistribute land to tenant farmers, although the success of these reforms varied by region.

2. Progressive Taxation and Social Welfare:

In more industrialized and modern societies, wealth redistribution has often been pursued through progressive taxation and the establishment of social welfare programs.

- **The Progressive Era (Late 19th to Early 20th Century)**: In the United States, the Progressive Era was marked by efforts to address the vast inequalities created by the Industrial Revolution. Progressive taxation, where the tax rate increases with income, became a key tool for redistributing wealth. The introduction of the federal income tax in 1913, and later the estate tax, were significant milestones in this effort. These taxes were designed to reduce the concentration of wealth by taxing the rich at higher rates and using the revenue to fund public goods and services.

- **The Welfare State (Mid-20th Century)**: After World War II, many Western countries, particularly in Europe, expanded their social welfare programs as part of the development of the welfare state. In the United Kingdom, the post-war Labour government implemented policies like the National Health Service (NHS) and expanded social security, funded by progressive taxation. These measures aimed to provide a safety net for all citizens and reduce the economic disparities that had characterized earlier periods.

- **Socialist Redistribution**: In socialist and communist countries, wealth redistribution was a central tenet of the political and economic system. The Soviet Union, for example, nationalized private property and wealth, redistributing it through state control of resources and centralized planning. While these policies did reduce some forms of economic inequality, they also led to inefficiencies and shortages, contributing to the eventual collapse of many socialist economies.

3. Inflationary and Deflationary Redistribution:

Economic policies affecting inflation and deflation have also served as indirect means of wealth redistribution.

- **Inflationary Redistribution**: Inflation can act as a form of wealth redistribution by eroding the value of money held by savers, who are typically wealthier, and reducing the real value of debt, which benefits debtors, often in lower-income brackets. Hyperinflation in Weimar Germany, for example, wiped out the savings of the middle class but also relieved many of their debts, leading to a significant redistribution of wealth.
- **Deflationary Redistribution**: Conversely, deflation increases the value of money and debt, benefiting creditors and those with substantial cash reserves while hurting debtors and those reliant on wage income. Deflationary policies, such as those implemented during the Great Depression, often exacerbated wealth inequality, as they tended to favor the wealthy over the working class.

Contemporary Options for Wealth Redistribution

1. Progressive Taxation and Closing Tax Loopholes:

Progressive taxation remains a cornerstone of wealth redistribution in contemporary economies. However, in recent decades, tax policies in many countries have become less progressive, with tax rates on the wealthy declining and tax avoidance strategies proliferating.

- **Increased Progressive Taxation**: Advocates for wealth redistribution argue for higher income taxes on the wealthy, increased capital gains taxes, and the reintroduction or strengthening of inheritance taxes. The aim is to reduce the wealth gap by ensuring that the richest individuals and corporations contribute a fairer share of their income to public revenue.
- **Closing Tax Loopholes**: Another important aspect is closing tax loopholes and combating tax evasion, which disproportionately benefit the wealthy. Global efforts to address tax havens and improve transparency in financial reporting are critical to ensuring that wealth is not hidden or shielded from taxation.

2. Universal Basic Income (UBI):

Universal Basic Income (UBI) has emerged as a modern proposal for wealth redistribution. UBI involves providing all citizens with a regular, unconditional cash payment, regardless of their income or employment status.

- **Rationale and Implementation**: Proponents argue that UBI can reduce poverty and inequality by ensuring a minimum income for everyone, enabling people to cover basic needs, pursue education, or start businesses. Pilot programs in countries like Finland and Kenya have tested the feasibility of UBI, with varying results. However, questions remain about the funding and long-term effects of such a program on work incentives and inflation.

- **Criticisms and Challenges**: Critics of UBI argue that it could be prohibitively expensive and might lead to reduced motivation to work. Additionally, some argue that targeted welfare programs might be more effective at addressing specific needs without the broad, universal approach of UBI.

3. Wealth Taxes:

Wealth taxes, distinct from income taxes, target the accumulated assets of the wealthy, including real estate, stocks, and other investments.

- **Implementation**: Countries like France and Spain have experimented with wealth taxes, though these have faced challenges such as capital flight and difficulties in accurately assessing wealth. In the United States, political figures like Elizabeth Warren and Bernie Sanders have proposed wealth taxes as a way to address extreme inequality.

- **Challenges**: The implementation of wealth taxes can be complex, requiring accurate valuation of assets and robust enforcement mechanisms. Critics argue that wealth taxes might discourage investment and lead to capital flight, where wealthy individuals move their assets to jurisdictions with lower taxes.

4. Expanding Social Safety Nets and Public Services:

Expanding and modernizing social safety nets is another approach to wealth redistribution. This includes universal healthcare, education, and housing policies that ensure access to essential services for all citizens.

- **Healthcare and Education**: Ensuring access to quality healthcare and education can level the playing field and provide opportunities for upward mobility. Publicly funded healthcare systems, like the NHS in the UK, and free or subsidized education are examples of how wealth can be redistributed by ensuring everyone has access to these fundamental services.
- **Housing and Infrastructure**: Investment in affordable housing and infrastructure, particularly in underserved communities, can also contribute to reducing wealth inequality. Policies that address housing shortages, improve public

transportation, and ensure access to clean water and energy are essential for redistributing wealth and improving quality of life for lower-income individuals.

5. Corporate Social Responsibility (CSR) and Ethical Investing:

CSR and ethical investing represent softer approaches to wealth redistribution, where corporations and investors voluntarily take steps to address inequality.

- **CSR Initiatives**: Companies engaging in CSR may invest in community development, pay fair wages, reduce environmental impact, and ensure ethical supply chains. While these actions can contribute to reducing inequality, their impact is often limited by the voluntary nature and varying commitment levels of corporations.
- **Ethical Investing**: Ethical investing involves directing capital toward companies and projects that prioritize social good, environmental sustainability, and ethical governance. By choosing to invest in businesses that align with these values, investors can indirectly influence wealth distribution by supporting practices that benefit a broader range of stakeholders.

Conclusion

Wealth redistribution has played a crucial role in shaping societies throughout history, addressing economic inequality and promoting social justice. Historical approaches, such as land reforms and progressive taxation, have left lasting legacies, while contemporary options like UBI, wealth taxes, and CSR offer new ways to tackle the challenges of inequality in the modern world. As economic disparities continue to grow, the debate over how best to redistribute wealth remains central to discussions about the future of economic policy and social equity. Understanding the strengths and weaknesses of various redistribution strategies is essential for crafting policies that foster a more just and equitable society.

Modern Causes of Poverty: An In-Depth Exploration

Introduction

Poverty remains a pervasive issue in the modern world, affecting billions of people across the globe. Despite advances in technology, economic growth, and increased global wealth, poverty continues to be a significant challenge for both developed and developing countries. Understanding the modern causes of poverty is essential for developing effective policies and strategies to combat it. This exploration delves into the multifaceted and interconnected causes of poverty in the 21st century, including economic inequality, unemployment, education, globalization, and systemic issues such as discrimination and governance.

1. Economic Inequality

Wealth and Income Disparities: One of the most significant modern causes of poverty is the growing disparity between the rich and the poor. Economic inequality, both within and between countries, has intensified in recent decades. The concentration of wealth in the hands of a small elite while large segments of the population struggle to meet basic needs has created a situation where economic growth benefits only a few, leaving many behind. Factors contributing to this inequality include tax policies favoring the wealthy, wage stagnation for low- and middle-income workers, and the rising cost of living.

Capital and Technology-Driven Economies: In modern economies, capital and technology have become central to wealth creation. Those who own capital, such as businesses, real estate, or financial assets, benefit disproportionately from economic growth. Meanwhile, those without access to capital or technology—often the poor—find it increasingly difficult to improve their economic standing. Automation and technological advancements have also displaced many low-skill jobs, exacerbating unemployment and underemployment among vulnerable populations.

2. Unemployment and Underemployment

Labor Market Changes: The shift from manufacturing to service-based economies in many countries has led to a decline in stable, well-paying jobs for low-skilled workers. This transition has left many without the necessary skills to compete in the modern job market, leading to unemployment or underemployment, where individuals are forced to accept jobs that are insecure, poorly paid, or part-time.

Globalization and Outsourcing: Globalization has led to the outsourcing of jobs from high-wage to low-wage countries, causing job losses in industries such as manufacturing in developed nations. While outsourcing can create jobs in developing countries, these jobs are often low-paying and lack labor protections, keeping workers in poverty. Moreover, the benefits of globalization are unevenly distributed, with wealthier individuals and corporations reaping the most rewards.

Informal Economy: In many developing countries, a significant portion of the workforce is employed in the informal economy, which includes jobs that are not regulated or protected by the state. Workers in the informal economy often lack job security, benefits, and legal protections, making them particularly vulnerable to poverty. The informal economy can perpetuate cycles of poverty, as workers are unable to access social safety nets or improve their living conditions.

3. Education and Skill Gaps

Access to Quality Education: Education is a key determinant of economic opportunities and upward mobility. However, access to quality education remains unequal, particularly in low-income and rural areas. Inadequate education systems fail to equip students with the skills needed for the modern workforce, trapping them in low-wage jobs or unemployment. The digital divide further exacerbates this issue, as those without access to technology are unable to acquire digital literacy skills essential in today's economy.

Rising Cost of Education: In many countries, the cost of higher education has skyrocketed, placing it out of reach for many low-income families. The burden of student debt can also limit economic mobility, as graduates are forced to allocate a significant portion of their income to loan repayments. This financial strain can prevent individuals from investing in their future, such as buying a home or starting a business, thereby perpetuating poverty.

4. Systemic Discrimination

Racial and Gender Inequality: Systemic discrimination based on race, gender, and other identity factors continues to be a significant cause of poverty. In many countries, minority groups and women face barriers to education, employment, and economic resources, limiting their opportunities for upward mobility. Wage gaps, discriminatory hiring practices, and limited access to capital for minority-owned businesses are some of the ways in which systemic discrimination contributes to poverty.

Social Exclusion: Social exclusion, where certain groups are marginalized and denied full participation in society, is closely linked to poverty. This can occur due to discrimination based on ethnicity, religion, disability, or immigration status. Socially excluded individuals often lack access to essential services, including healthcare, education, and housing, making it difficult for them to escape poverty.

5. Governance and Political Factors

Corruption and Poor Governance: Corruption and poor governance are significant contributors to poverty, particularly in developing countries. When government officials misappropriate public funds or engage in corrupt practices, resources that should be used to improve public services, infrastructure, and social welfare programs are instead diverted to private interests. This deprives citizens of the necessary support to escape poverty and undermines trust in public institutions.

Weak Social Safety Nets: Inadequate social safety nets are a major cause of poverty in both developed and developing countries. Social safety nets, such as unemployment benefits, healthcare, and food assistance, are designed to protect individuals from falling into poverty during times of economic hardship.

However, in many countries, these programs are underfunded, poorly implemented, or non-existent, leaving vulnerable populations without a safety net.

Political Instability and Conflict: Political instability and conflict are also major drivers of poverty. War and violence can displace populations, destroy infrastructure, and disrupt economic activity, leading to widespread poverty. Additionally, political instability can deter investment and economic development, further exacerbating poverty.

6. Health and Environmental Factors

Health Inequities: Poor health is both a cause and a consequence of poverty. Individuals in poverty often lack access to healthcare, leading to untreated illnesses and disabilities that can prevent them from working or achieving economic stability. Health crises, such as the HIV/AIDS epidemic or the COVID-19 pandemic, disproportionately affect the poor, exacerbating existing inequalities.

Environmental Degradation and Climate Change: Environmental factors, including climate change and natural disasters, can also contribute to poverty. Communities that rely on agriculture, fishing, or other natural resources for their livelihoods are particularly vulnerable to environmental changes. Climate change can lead to crop failures, water shortages, and extreme weather events, pushing already vulnerable populations further into poverty. Additionally, environmental degradation, such as deforestation and pollution, can reduce access to essential resources like clean water and arable land, exacerbating poverty.

Conclusion

Poverty in the modern world is the result of a complex interplay of economic, social, and political factors. While economic inequality, unemployment, and inadequate education are key contributors, systemic discrimination, poor governance, and health disparities also play significant roles. Addressing modern poverty requires a multifaceted approach that includes policies aimed at reducing economic inequality, improving access to quality education and healthcare, strengthening social safety nets, and combating discrimination. Only by tackling these root causes can we hope to reduce poverty and create a more equitable and just society for all.

Fierce Egalitarianism: A Deep Dive into Radical Equality

Introduction

Fierce egalitarianism is a concept rooted in the unwavering commitment to achieving and maintaining equality across all dimensions of society. Unlike more moderate approaches that might advocate for incremental changes or accept certain levels of inequality as inevitable, fierce egalitarianism demands radical and comprehensive measures to ensure that every individual has equal access to resources, opportunities, and rights. This ideology, often associated with leftist political movements, challenges deeply entrenched power structures and advocates for a society where disparities in wealth, status, and privilege are entirely eradicated. This exploration delves into the principles of fierce egalitarianism, its historical roots, and its implications for modern society.

1. Defining Fierce Egalitarianism

Core Principles: Fierce egalitarianism is characterized by a relentless pursuit of equality in all its forms—economic, social, political, and cultural. It rejects any form of hierarchy or privilege that elevates one group over another. This ideology is based on the belief that all individuals should have equal access to resources and opportunities, regardless of their background, identity, or circumstances.

At its core, fierce egalitarianism is about dismantling systems of oppression and inequality. It goes beyond merely advocating for equal rights or opportunities and seeks to actively redistribute power and resources to achieve true equality. This often involves challenging existing social norms, institutions, and practices that perpetuate inequality, and replacing them with systems that promote fairness and inclusivity.

Economic Equality: In the economic realm, fierce egalitarianism demands a radical redistribution of wealth and resources. This includes not only addressing income inequality but also ensuring that all individuals have access to basic needs such as housing, healthcare, education, and food. It often calls for the abolition of private property or the implementation of communal ownership models, where resources are shared equitably among all members of society.

Fierce egalitarians argue that economic inequality is not only a moral failing but also a root cause of other forms of inequality. By concentrating wealth in the hands of a few, societies create power imbalances that allow the wealthy to dominate political and social institutions. Fierce egalitarianism seeks to eliminate these imbalances by redistributing wealth and creating a society where everyone has equal access to economic resources.

Social and Cultural Equality: Socially and culturally, fierce egalitarianism advocates for the dismantling of all forms of discrimination and privilege, including those based on race, gender, sexuality, religion, and other identity markers. It emphasizes the need for intersectionality, recognizing that individuals often experience multiple, overlapping forms of oppression. To achieve true equality, fierce egalitarianism calls for the complete elimination of social hierarchies and the creation of a society where all individuals are valued equally.

In this context, fierce egalitarianism often involves challenging cultural norms and practices that reinforce inequality. For example, it might involve advocating for gender-neutral language, promoting inclusive education that reflects diverse perspectives, or challenging media representations that perpetuate stereotypes. Fierce egalitarianism seeks to create a culture where diversity is celebrated, and everyone has the freedom to express their identity without fear of discrimination or marginalization.

Political Equality: Politically, fierce egalitarianism advocates for the equal distribution of power and decision-making authority. This often involves supporting direct democracy or other forms of participatory governance, where all individuals have an equal say in decisions that affect their lives. Fierce egalitarians reject systems where power is concentrated in the hands of a few, whether through elected representatives, political elites, or corporate interests.

In practice, political equality under fierce egalitarianism might involve reforms such as proportional representation, the elimination of electoral districts that disproportionately favor certain groups, or the introduction of mechanisms for direct citizen participation in policymaking. Fierce egalitarians believe that political power should be distributed equally among all members of society, ensuring that everyone's voice is heard and valued.

2. Historical Roots of Fierce Egalitarianism

Indigenous Societies: The concept of fierce egalitarianism can be traced back to various indigenous societies that practiced forms of communal living and decision-making. Many indigenous cultures emphasized collective ownership of resources, consensus-based decision-making, and the equal distribution of wealth and power. These societies often rejected hierarchical structures and instead valued cooperation and mutual support. For example, some hunter-gatherer societies are known for their strict adherence to egalitarian principles, where resources are shared equally among all members of the community.

Religious and Philosophical Traditions: Fierce egalitarianism has also been influenced by various religious and philosophical traditions that advocate for radical equality. For example, early Christian communities practiced forms of communal living and wealth sharing, inspired by teachings that emphasized the inherent worth of all individuals and the need to care for the poor and marginalized. Similarly, the principles of fierce egalitarianism can be found in the teachings of various Eastern philosophies, such as Buddhism, which advocates for compassion, non-attachment, and the rejection of material wealth as a source of inequality.

Revolutionary Movements: In more recent history, fierce egalitarianism has been a driving force behind various revolutionary movements that sought to overthrow oppressive regimes and create more equal societies. The French Revolution, for example, was driven by ideals of "liberté, égalité, fraternité," and sought to eliminate the privileges of the aristocracy and create a more equal society. Similarly, the socialist and communist movements of the 19th and 20th centuries were inspired by the belief that true equality could only be achieved through the abolition of private property and the establishment of a classless society.

While many of these movements were not fully successful in achieving their goals, they have left a lasting legacy and continue to inspire contemporary advocates of fierce egalitarianism. The struggles for workers' rights, women's suffrage, civil rights, and other social justice movements have all been influenced by the principles of fierce egalitarianism and have contributed to the ongoing fight for equality.

3. Implications for Modern Society

Challenges to Implementation: While the ideals of fierce egalitarianism are appealing to many, implementing these principles in modern society poses significant challenges. Fierce egalitarianism often requires radical changes to existing social, economic, and political systems, which can be difficult to achieve in practice. Moreover, the concentration of wealth and power in the hands of a few can make it challenging to build the broad-based coalitions needed to enact such changes.

Additionally, fierce egalitarianism often faces opposition from those who benefit from the current system of inequality. Efforts to redistribute wealth or power are frequently met with resistance from wealthy individuals, corporations, and political elites who seek to maintain their privileged positions. This resistance can manifest in various ways, including lobbying against progressive policies, spreading misinformation, or using legal and political mechanisms to undermine efforts toward equality.

Potential for Social Change: Despite these challenges, fierce egalitarianism offers a powerful vision for social change. By challenging existing power structures and advocating for radical equality, fierce egalitarians can help to create a more just and equitable society. This might involve building grassroots movements that advocate for economic justice, supporting policies that promote wealth redistribution, or working to dismantle systems of discrimination and privilege.

Moreover, fierce egalitarianism can serve as a moral and ethical guide for individuals and communities seeking to create a more equal world. By prioritizing equality and rejecting all forms of hierarchy and oppression, fierce egalitarians can inspire others to take action and work toward a society where everyone has an equal chance to thrive.

Global Implications: Fierce egalitarianism also has significant implications at the global level. In an increasingly interconnected world, global inequality has become a pressing issue, with vast disparities in wealth, resources, and opportunities between different countries and regions. Fierce egalitarians advocate for global justice, calling for the redistribution of resources and the establishment of international systems that promote equality and protect the rights of all people, regardless of where they live.

This might involve advocating for fair trade policies, supporting global efforts to combat climate change and environmental degradation, or working to ensure that all people have access to essential resources like clean water, healthcare, and education. Fierce egalitarians believe that true equality cannot be achieved within individual countries alone but must be pursued at a global level, ensuring that everyone, regardless of nationality, can enjoy the benefits of a just and equitable world.

Conclusion

Rooted in historical traditions and revolutionary movements, Fierce egalitarianism challenges the status quo and advocates for radical changes to economic, social, and political systems. While implementing fierce egalitarianism in modern society presents significant challenges, its potential to create a more just and equitable world is undeniable. By prioritizing equality and working to dismantle systems of oppression, fierce egalitarians offer a powerful vision for a society where everyone has the opportunity to thrive, free from the constraints of inequality and discrimination.

Social Contract Theory: Foundations and Evolution

Introduction

Social contract theory is a cornerstone of political philosophy, proposing that the legitimacy of government and the authority of rulers are derived from an implicit contract between the governed and those who govern. This theory has been a pivotal concept in the development of modern political thought, influencing the structure of societies, the formation of governments, and the rights and duties of citizens. Rooted in the works of early modern philosophers such as Thomas Hobbes, John Locke, and Jean-Jacques Rousseau, social contract theory continues to be relevant today as it provides a framework for understanding the relationship between individuals and the state, and the principles underlying justice, rights, and democracy.

1. Foundations of Social Contract Theory

Origins and Key Thinkers: Social contract theory emerged during the Enlightenment, a period marked by the questioning of traditional authority and the exploration of new ideas about governance and human nature. The theory is grounded in the idea that individuals in a state of nature—where there is no formal government—would naturally come together to form a society and establish rules for mutual benefit. The "social contract" is the agreement by which individuals consent to give up some of their freedoms and submit to an authority in exchange for protection of their remaining rights and maintenance of social order.

- **Thomas Hobbes (1588–1679):** Hobbes is often considered the father of social contract theory. In his seminal work, *Leviathan* (1651), he argued that in the state of nature, human life would be "solitary, poor, nasty, brutish, and short." To escape this chaotic and dangerous existence, individuals would agree to form a commonwealth, governed by a sovereign with absolute authority. For Hobbes, the social contract justified the establishment of a powerful government to ensure peace and security, even at the cost of some individual freedoms.
- **John Locke (1632–1704):** Locke's version of the social contract, as articulated in his *Two Treatises of Government* (1689), contrasts sharply with Hobbes'. Locke viewed the state of nature more optimistically, seeing individuals as rational and capable of self-governance. However, to protect their natural rights—life, liberty, and property— individuals would consent to form a government with limited powers. Unlike Hobbes, Locke argued that government authority is not absolute

and that individuals retain the right to overthrow a government that fails to protect their rights. This idea laid the groundwork for modern democracy and constitutional government.

- **Jean-Jacques Rousseau (1712–1778):** Rousseau further developed social contract theory in his work *The Social Contract* (1762). He posited that in the state of nature, humans were noble savages, living free and equal. The advent of private property, however, led to inequality and social strife. Rousseau proposed that the social contract should be based on the "general will," or the collective will of the people, which represents the common good. Unlike Hobbes and Locke, Rousseau emphasized direct democracy and the idea that sovereignty resides with the people, not with a monarch or government.

Core Concepts: Social contract theory revolves around several key concepts:

- **State of Nature:** A hypothetical condition in which individuals live without a formal government or laws. The state of nature is used by social contract theorists to illustrate the need for organized society and government.
- **Consent of the Governed:** The idea that government derives its legitimacy from the

consent of the people it governs. This consent is given either explicitly, through acts like voting, or implicitly, by participating in society and obeying its laws.

- **Natural Rights:** Fundamental rights that individuals possess in the state of nature. These rights, such as life, liberty, and property, are considered inalienable and must be protected by the government.
- **General Will:** Rousseau's concept of the collective will of the people, which represents the common good. The general will is the basis of legitimate government authority in Rousseau's social contract.
- **Sovereignty:** The ultimate authority to govern, which, according to different theorists, can reside in a monarch (Hobbes), the people (Rousseau), or a combination of both (Locke).

2. Evolution and Impact of Social Contract Theory

Development and Criticisms: Social contract theory has evolved over time, with various thinkers building on or critiquing the ideas of Hobbes, Locke, and Rousseau. In the 18th and 19th centuries, social contract theory influenced the development of constitutional democracy, particularly in the American and French revolutions. The U.S. Declaration of

Independence and Constitution, for example, reflect Locke's ideas about natural rights and government by consent.

However, social contract theory has also faced criticisms. Some critics argue that the theory is based on a fictional or idealized account of human nature and history. The state of nature, for example, is a hypothetical construct rather than a historical reality. Feminist and critical race theorists have critiqued social contract theory for its exclusion of women, people of color, and other marginalized groups, who were often not considered full participants in the social contract. These critiques have led to the development of alternative theories that seek to address these shortcomings.

Contemporary Relevance: Despite these criticisms, social contract theory remains relevant in contemporary political philosophy and legal theory. It continues to provide a foundation for discussions about the legitimacy of government, the rights and duties of citizens, and the principles of justice. In modern democracies, the idea of government by consent of the governed is a central tenet, and social contract theory offers a framework for understanding the relationship between individuals and the state.

Social contract theory also informs debates about social justice, economic inequality, and human rights. For example, discussions about the role of government in providing healthcare, education, and social services often draw on the idea that individuals have a collective responsibility to support one another through the social contract. Similarly, the concept of the general will is invoked in discussions about the common good and the balance between individual rights and collective responsibilities.

Applications in Law and Governance: In legal theory, social contract principles underpin the rule of law and constitutionalism. Constitutions, as foundational legal documents, can be seen as expressions of the social contract, outlining the rights and responsibilities of citizens and the limits of government power. Courts often interpret constitutional provisions in light of social contract principles, ensuring that government actions are consistent with the consent of the governed and the protection of natural rights.

Social contract theory also influences contemporary governance practices, such as the design of democratic institutions, the protection of civil liberties, and the promotion of social welfare. For instance, debates about the balance between security and individual freedom in the context of counterterrorism measures often reference social contract ideas, weighing the need for government authority against the protection of individual rights.

Global Implications: Beyond national borders, social contract theory has implications for international relations and global governance. The idea of a global social contract has been proposed as a way to address global challenges such as climate change, poverty, and human rights abuses. Advocates of a global social contract argue that just as individuals consent to be governed within a state, nations and peoples should cooperate globally to achieve common goals and protect global public goods.

This global perspective on the social contract also raises questions about sovereignty, international law, and global justice. For example, the United Nations and other international institutions can be seen as attempts to create a global social contract, where nations agree to adhere to common rules and standards in exchange for the benefits of international cooperation and peace.

Conclusion

Social contract theory is a foundational concept in political philosophy that has shaped the development of modern political thought and governance. From its origins in the works of Hobbes, Locke, and Rousseau, the theory has evolved to address contemporary challenges and continues to influence debates about the legitimacy of government, the rights of citizens, and the principles of justice. While the theory has faced criticisms and undergone significant reinterpretation, its core ideas remain relevant in discussions about democracy, human rights, and global governance. As societies continue to grapple with issues of inequality, social justice, and the role of government, social contract theory offers a valuable framework for understanding the relationship between individuals and the state, and the responsibilities we share as members of a political community.

For-Profit Healthcare vs. Socialized Medicine: A Comparative Analysis

Introduction

Healthcare systems around the world are structured in various ways, with two predominant models being for-profit healthcare and socialized medicine. These systems reflect different philosophical approaches to healthcare delivery, financing, and the role of government. For-profit healthcare is largely driven by market forces and emphasizes individual choice and competition, while socialized medicine prioritizes universal access, government responsibility, and the collective good. This contrast in approaches significantly affects how healthcare is provided, who has access, and how it is funded. This analysis explores the key differences between for-profit healthcare and socialized medicine, examining their respective advantages, disadvantages, and implications for society.

1. For-Profit Healthcare: Market-Driven and Competitive

Structure and Principles: For-profit healthcare is a system where healthcare services are provided by private entities, including hospitals, clinics, insurance companies, and pharmaceutical firms, that operate for profit. The guiding principle of this system is that competition in the marketplace leads to innovation, efficiency, and improved quality of care. Patients, as consumers, are believed to benefit from having a variety of choices in providers and services, with the assumption that market competition will drive down costs and enhance quality.

In this model, healthcare is treated as a commodity, with access to services largely determined by an individual's ability to pay. Health insurance, whether provided by employers, purchased individually, or obtained through government programs, plays a crucial role in determining who can access care and what kind of care they receive. In countries like the United States, for-profit healthcare is the dominant model, with a mix of private and public insurance programs.

Advantages of For-Profit Healthcare:

1. **Innovation and Technological Advancement:** The profit motive in healthcare drives competition among providers and companies, leading to innovation in medical technology, treatments, and pharmaceuticals. The pursuit of profit can incentivize research and development, resulting in advanced medical practices and cutting-edge technologies.
2. **Consumer Choice:** For-profit healthcare systems offer patients a wide range of choices in

providers, treatments, and insurance plans. This flexibility allows individuals to select the care that best suits their needs and preferences, theoretically leading to a more personalized healthcare experience.

3. **Efficiency through Competition:** Market competition encourages efficiency among providers. Hospitals and clinics must operate effectively to attract patients and remain profitable. This competition can lead to better service, shorter wait times, and improved overall patient care.

Disadvantages of For-Profit Healthcare:

1. **Inequality in Access:** One of the primary criticisms of for-profit healthcare is that it creates significant disparities in access to care. Individuals with higher incomes or comprehensive insurance coverage can afford better care, while those without sufficient resources may face barriers to accessing necessary services, leading to unequal health outcomes.

2. **High Costs:** Despite the emphasis on competition, for-profit healthcare systems can be expensive. Administrative costs, profit margins, and the high price of medical services and

insurance can contribute to rising healthcare expenses, making it difficult for many people to afford care.

3. **Focus on Profit Over Patient Care:** The profit-driven nature of this system can sometimes prioritize financial outcomes over patient well-being. Hospitals and providers may focus on lucrative procedures and treatments rather than preventive care or addressing the needs of less profitable patient populations.

4. **Complexity and Fragmentation:** For-profit healthcare systems often involve multiple private insurers, each with different coverage options, networks, and regulations. This can lead to a complex and fragmented system that is difficult for patients to navigate, often resulting in confusion and inefficiency.

2. Socialized Medicine: Universal Access and Government Responsibility

Structure and Principles: Socialized medicine refers to a healthcare system where the government plays a central role in financing and delivering healthcare services. In this model, healthcare is considered a public good, and the government ensures that all citizens have access to necessary medical care, regardless of their ability to pay. Socialized medicine is funded primarily through taxation, and healthcare providers are often employed by the state or operate under government contracts. This model is exemplified by systems such as the National Health Service (NHS) in the United Kingdom.

The underlying philosophy of socialized medicine is that healthcare is a fundamental human right, and the state has a responsibility to ensure that all citizens receive equitable care. This approach emphasizes the collective well-being of society and seeks to eliminate barriers to healthcare access.

Advantages of Socialized Medicine:

1. **Universal Access:** One of the most significant advantages of socialized medicine is that it provides universal access to healthcare. Every citizen, regardless of income, has access to a comprehensive range of medical services, ensuring that no one is excluded from care due to financial constraints.

2. **Equity in Health Outcomes:** By eliminating the financial barriers to care, socialized medicine promotes greater equity in health outcomes. Disparities in health based on income or social status are reduced, contributing to a healthier overall population.

3. **Cost Control:** Socialized medicine systems are often able to control costs more effectively than for-profit systems. Centralized negotiation for drug prices, standardized care protocols, and the elimination of profit-driven pricing contribute to lower overall healthcare expenditures.

4. **Focus on Preventive Care:** Socialized medicine places a strong emphasis on preventive care and public health initiatives. By prioritizing early intervention and disease prevention, these systems can reduce the long-term costs associated with chronic conditions and improve population health.

Disadvantages of Socialized Medicine:

1. **Potential for Long Wait Times:** One common criticism of socialized medicine is the potential for longer wait times for certain procedures and treatments. Limited resources and high demand can lead to delays in receiving care, particularly for non-urgent or elective procedures.

2. **Limited Consumer Choice:** In socialized medicine systems, patients may have fewer choices when it comes to selecting healthcare providers or treatments. Government regulations and standardized care protocols can restrict

options, which some individuals may find limiting.

3. **Bureaucratic Inefficiencies:** The centralized nature of socialized medicine can lead to bureaucratic inefficiencies. Large government-run systems may be slower to adapt to changes or innovations, and administrative processes can be cumbersome.

4. **Taxation and Public Funding:** Socialized medicine is funded through taxation, which can be a contentious issue. Higher taxes may be required to sustain the system, and there is ongoing debate about the appropriate level of government spending on healthcare.

3. Societal Implications and Ethical Considerations

Ethical Considerations: The debate between for-profit healthcare and socialized medicine often hinges on differing ethical perspectives. Proponents of for-profit healthcare argue that individual freedom and choice are paramount, and that competition and market forces are the best mechanisms for delivering high-quality care. They may also contend that individuals should be responsible for their own health and well-being, and that the government should play a limited role in healthcare.

On the other hand, advocates of socialized medicine emphasize the ethical principle of equity and the belief that healthcare is a fundamental right. They argue that society has a collective responsibility to ensure that everyone has access to necessary medical care, regardless of their financial circumstances. This perspective often prioritizes the common good over individual choice, and sees the government as a necessary guarantor of health equity.

Social and Economic Implications: The choice between for-profit healthcare and socialized medicine has profound social and economic implications. For-profit systems can lead to greater economic inequality, as access to care is often tied to wealth and income. This can result in significant disparities in health outcomes, with marginalized and low-income populations experiencing worse health and shorter lifespans.

In contrast, socialized medicine systems aim to reduce these disparities by providing universal access to care. However, these systems require substantial public investment and may face challenges related to funding, efficiency, and resource allocation.

The economic impact of these systems also varies. For-profit healthcare can drive economic growth in sectors like pharmaceuticals and medical technology, but it can also lead to high healthcare costs and financial strain on individuals. Socialized medicine, while potentially less costly overall, requires sustainable public funding and effective management to avoid issues like underfunding and resource shortages.

Conclusion

The debate between for-profit healthcare and socialized medicine reflects broader societal values and priorities. For-profit healthcare emphasizes individual choice, market-driven innovation, and competition, but it can also lead to significant inequalities in access and outcomes. Socialized medicine, on the other hand, prioritizes universal access, equity, and government responsibility, but it may face challenges related to efficiency, funding, and patient choice. Ultimately, the choice between these models depends on how a society balances the principles of individual freedom, equity, and collective responsibility in the pursuit of health and well-being for all its citizens.

Socialized Education: Foundations, Principles, and Implications

Introduction

Socialized education refers to an educational system that is primarily funded, regulated, and operated by the government, with the aim of providing equal access to quality education for all members of society. This concept is rooted in the belief that education is a fundamental human right and that the state has a responsibility to ensure that every individual, regardless of socio-economic background, has the opportunity to receive an education. Socialized education systems are characterized by universal access, public funding, standardized curricula, and a focus on promoting social equity and cohesion. This analysis explores the foundations of socialized education, its guiding principles, the advantages and challenges it presents, and its broader implications for society.

1. Foundations and Principles of Socialized Education

Historical Context: The concept of socialized education has its roots in the Enlightenment era when thinkers like Jean-Jacques Rousseau and John Locke began advocating for the importance of education in the development of individuals and societies. The idea gained traction in the 19th and 20th centuries, particularly in the context of industrialization and the rise of nation-states, where there was a growing recognition that an educated populace was essential for economic development, social stability, and democratic governance.

In many countries, the establishment of socialized education systems was a response to the inequalities and limitations of private and religious education, which often excluded large segments of the population, particularly the poor and marginalized. Governments began to see education as a public good, necessary for both individual advancement and the collective well-being of society.

Guiding Principles: Socialized education is guided by several key principles:

1. **Universal Access:** The cornerstone of socialized education is the principle of universal access, which ensures that every child, regardless of their socio-economic background, has the right to receive a quality education. This principle is enshrined in the constitutions and legal frameworks of many countries and is often implemented through compulsory education laws that mandate school attendance for children up to a certain age.

2. **Public Funding:** Socialized education systems are primarily funded through taxation, which allows for the distribution of educational resources based on need rather than ability to pay. This public funding model aims to reduce disparities in educational opportunities and ensure that all schools, regardless of their location or the wealth of their communities, have the resources necessary to provide a high-quality education.

3. **Standardization and Equality:** To promote fairness and social cohesion, socialized education systems often emphasize standardization in curricula, teacher qualifications, and school facilities. This standardization seeks to ensure that all students, regardless of where they live or which school they attend, receive a similar quality of education and are held to the same academic standards.

4. **Social Equity:** Socialized education aims to address social inequalities by providing additional support to disadvantaged students and communities. This may include targeted funding for schools in low-income areas, special education programs, and initiatives to close achievement gaps based on race, ethnicity, gender, or disability.

5. **Democratic Citizenship:** A key goal of socialized education is to prepare students to participate fully in democratic society. This includes not only providing them with the knowledge and skills needed to succeed in the workforce but also fostering critical thinking, civic responsibility, and an understanding of social and political issues.

2. Advantages of Socialized Education

Promoting Social Equity and Inclusion: One of the most significant advantages of socialized education is its potential to promote social equity and inclusion. By providing universal access to education, socialized systems help to level the playing field for students from diverse socio-economic backgrounds. Public funding ensures that even students from low-income families have access to quality education, reducing the risk of intergenerational poverty and social exclusion.

Economic Benefits: Socialized education also offers substantial economic benefits. An educated workforce is essential for economic growth and development, as it increases productivity, innovation, and the overall competitiveness of a nation. By investing in education, governments can help to ensure that all citizens have the skills and knowledge needed to participate in the economy, thereby reducing unemployment and underemployment.

Additionally, socialized education can lead to a more equitable distribution of wealth, as it provides individuals with the opportunity to improve their socio-economic status through education. This can help to reduce income inequality and promote social mobility, contributing to a more stable and cohesive society.

Enhancing Democratic Participation: Socialized education plays a critical role in enhancing democratic participation. By educating citizens about their rights and responsibilities, and fostering critical thinking and civic engagement, socialized education systems help to create an informed electorate that is capable of participating effectively in the democratic process. This is particularly important in ensuring that all voices are heard in a democracy, including those of marginalized or disadvantaged groups.

Improving Public Health and Social Outcomes: Education is closely linked to a range of positive social outcomes, including better health, lower crime rates, and higher levels of civic participation. Socialized education systems, by ensuring that all individuals have access to education, contribute to these positive outcomes, leading to a healthier, safer, and more engaged society.

3. Challenges and Criticisms of Socialized Education

Resource Constraints and Funding Challenges: One of the primary challenges facing socialized education systems is the issue of funding. Public education systems rely heavily on government funding, which can be subject to political and economic fluctuations. In times of economic downturn or austerity, education budgets may be cut, leading to larger class sizes, outdated materials, and underpaid teachers. These resource constraints can undermine the quality of education and exacerbate inequalities, particularly in underfunded schools.

Bureaucracy and Inefficiency: Another common criticism of socialized education is the potential for bureaucracy and inefficiency. Large, government-run education systems can be slow to adapt to new challenges and innovations, and may suffer from rigid administrative structures that limit the ability of schools to respond to the specific needs of their students. This can lead to a one-size-fits-all approach that may not be effective in addressing the diverse needs of a modern student population.

Standardization vs. Individualization: While standardization is intended to ensure fairness and equality, it can also be seen as a limitation in socialized education systems. Critics argue that an overly standardized approach to education can stifle creativity, innovation, and the ability to tailor education to the unique needs of individual students. There is a tension between the need to provide a consistent quality of education and the desire to foster personalized learning experiences that cater to different learning styles and interests.

Political Influence and Control: Socialized education systems are often subject to political influence and control, which can impact the content of curricula, the allocation of resources, and the overall direction of education policy. This can lead to the politicization of education, where decisions about what is taught in schools are influenced by political ideologies rather than educational best practices. This can result in controversies over issues such as the teaching of history, science, and social studies, as well as debates over school choice and the role of private education.

4. Broader Implications and Future Considerations

Global Implications: The principles of socialized education have global implications, particularly in the context of efforts to achieve universal education as outlined in international agreements like the United Nations Sustainable Development Goals. Socialized education models can serve as a blueprint for developing countries seeking to expand access to education and improve educational outcomes. However, the challenges faced by these systems, particularly in terms of funding and resource allocation, must be carefully considered and addressed.

Balancing Public and Private Roles: As societies continue to evolve, there is ongoing debate about the appropriate balance between public and private roles in education. Some argue that a mixed system, where public education is complemented by private and charter schools, can offer a more diverse range of educational options and foster innovation. Others maintain that the core principles of socialized education—universal access, public funding, and equity—must remain central to ensure that education serves the common good rather than becoming a commodity accessible only to those who can afford it.

Adapting to the Future of Education: Looking to the future, socialized education systems must adapt to new challenges and opportunities, including the rapid pace of technological change, the increasing diversity of student populations, and the growing demand for skills-based education. This will require flexibility, innovation, and a commitment to maintaining the core values of equity, access, and social responsibility that underpin socialized education.

Conclusion

Socialized education represents a commitment to the idea that education is a fundamental right and a public good that should be accessible to all members of society. By providing universal access, public funding, and a focus on social equity, socialized education systems have the potential to promote social cohesion, economic development, and democratic participation. However, these systems also face significant challenges, including resource constraints, bureaucratic inefficiencies, and the need to balance standardization with individualization. As societies continue to grapple with these challenges, the principles of socialized education will remain central to discussions about the future of education and the role it plays in shaping a just and equitable society.

Housing as a Human Right: Foundations, Challenges, and Implications

Introduction

The concept of housing as a human right is rooted in the belief that every individual should have access to safe, secure, and adequate shelter. This idea is not merely a matter of providing physical space for living but is also intricately tied to dignity, health, social inclusion, and economic security. Housing as a human right implies that governments and societies have an obligation to ensure that all people, regardless of their socio-economic status, have access to decent housing. This principle has been recognized in various international human rights documents, including the Universal Declaration of Human Rights (UDHR) and the International Covenant on Economic, Social, and Cultural Rights (ICESCR). Despite these commitments, the realization of this right remains a significant challenge globally. This analysis explores the foundations of housing as a human right, the obstacles to its realization, and the broader implications for society.

1. Foundations of Housing as a Human Right

International Recognition: The recognition of housing as a human right can be traced back to the aftermath of

World War II, when the United Nations sought to establish a framework for promoting and protecting human dignity. Article 25 of the UDHR, adopted in 1948, states that "everyone has the right to a standard of living adequate for the health and well-being of himself and of his family, including food, clothing, housing, and medical care." This declaration laid the groundwork for subsequent international agreements and national policies aimed at ensuring access to adequate housing for all.

The ICESCR, adopted in 1966, further elaborates on the right to housing, stating in Article 11 that "the States Parties to the present Covenant recognize the right of everyone to an adequate standard of living for himself and his family, including adequate food, clothing, and housing, and to the continuous improvement of living conditions." This covenant obligates states to take appropriate steps to realize this right, including the adoption of legislative measures and the allocation of resources.

Key Elements of the Right to Housing: The right to housing encompasses several key elements that go beyond mere access to a physical dwelling. These elements, as outlined by the UN Committee on Economic, Social, and Cultural Rights, include:

1. **Security of Tenure:** Individuals should have legal protection against forced evictions, harassment, and other threats that undermine their right to secure housing. This protection applies to all forms of tenure, including rental housing, cooperative housing, and owner-occupied housing.
2. **Availability of Services, Materials, Facilities, and Infrastructure:** Adequate housing must include access to essential services and facilities, such as clean water, sanitation, electricity, and heating. These services are vital for maintaining a safe and healthy living environment.
3. **Affordability:** Housing costs should be at a level that allows individuals to meet other basic needs, such as food, education, and healthcare. Governments have a responsibility to ensure that housing is affordable for all segments of the population, particularly low-income and vulnerable groups.
4. **Habitability:** Housing must provide adequate space, protection from the elements, and a safe and healthy environment. This includes ensuring that dwellings are structurally sound, free from hazards, and located in areas that are not prone to environmental risks, such as flooding or pollution.

5. **Accessibility:** Housing must be accessible to all individuals, including those with disabilities, the elderly, and other marginalized groups. This requires the removal of physical and societal barriers that prevent people from accessing adequate housing.

6. **Location:** Adequate housing should be located in areas that provide access to employment opportunities, education, healthcare, and other essential services. It should also be situated in environments that promote social inclusion and community participation.

7. **Cultural Adequacy:** Housing should respect the cultural identity and diversity of residents. This includes accommodating different cultural practices, traditions, and ways of life in the design and allocation of housing.

2. Challenges to the Realization of the Right to Housing

Global Housing Crisis: Despite the international recognition of housing as a human right, the global housing crisis remains a significant challenge. Millions of people around the world live in inadequate housing conditions, including slums, informal settlements, and overcrowded or substandard dwellings. The rapid urbanization of the 21st century has exacerbated this crisis, particularly in developing countries, where the demand for affordable housing far outstrips supply.

In many urban areas, the rising cost of land and housing has pushed low-income families to the margins of society, forcing them to live in unsafe and unsanitary conditions. Additionally, the financialization of housing—where housing is treated as a commodity and an investment rather than a basic human need—has led to increased housing prices and the displacement of vulnerable populations.

Homelessness: Homelessness is perhaps the most visible manifestation of the failure to realize the right to housing. In many cities across the world, homelessness has reached crisis levels, with growing numbers of people living on the streets, in shelters, or in precarious housing situations. The causes of homelessness are complex and multifaceted, including factors such as poverty, unemployment, mental health issues, and the lack of affordable housing.

Governments and social service agencies often struggle to address the needs of homeless populations, and many individuals who are homeless face significant barriers to accessing housing, including discrimination, inadequate social support systems, and the criminalization of homelessness.

Discrimination and Inequality: Discrimination and inequality are significant barriers to the realization of the right to housing. In many societies, marginalized groups—including racial and ethnic minorities, immigrants, people with disabilities, and LGBTQ+ individuals—face systemic discrimination in housing markets. This can take the form of exclusionary zoning practices, discriminatory lending practices, and unequal access to public housing programs.

In addition, women and children are disproportionately affected by housing insecurity. Women, particularly single mothers and survivors of domestic violence, often face challenges in securing adequate housing due to economic disadvantage, gender-based discrimination, and a lack of targeted support services.

Political and Economic Obstacles: Political and economic factors also play a critical role in shaping housing policy and the realization of the right to housing. In many countries, housing policies are influenced by market forces and the interests of private developers and investors, leading to a focus on profit-driven housing development rather than the provision of affordable and adequate housing for all.

Austerity measures, budget cuts, and the privatization of public housing have further undermined efforts to address housing needs, particularly in low-income communities. Additionally, corruption and mismanagement in housing programs can result in the diversion of resources away from those who need them most.

3. Implications and Future Considerations

The Role of Government and Policy: To effectively realize the right to housing, governments must take a proactive role in shaping housing policy and ensuring that housing is accessible, affordable, and adequate for all. This requires a commitment to social justice and equity, as well as the political will to address the root causes of housing insecurity and homelessness.

Policy measures that can support the realization of the right to housing include:

1. **Investing in Affordable Housing:** Governments must prioritize the development of affordable housing, particularly in urban areas where the demand is highest. This may involve direct public investment in housing construction, subsidies for low-income renters and homeowners, and the expansion of public housing programs.
2. **Strengthening Legal Protections:** Legal frameworks should be strengthened to protect

individuals' rights to secure tenure and to prevent discrimination in housing markets. This includes enforcing anti-discrimination laws, providing legal aid for those facing eviction, and ensuring that housing policies are inclusive of marginalized groups.

3. **Regulating the Housing Market:** To prevent the commodification of housing and the displacement of vulnerable populations, governments may need to implement regulations on rent control, property speculation, and the financialization of housing. These measures can help to stabilize housing markets and ensure that housing remains accessible to all.

4. **Supporting Vulnerable Populations:** Targeted support services, including emergency shelter, transitional housing, and social services, are essential for addressing the needs of homeless and housing-insecure populations. Governments should also focus on preventing homelessness by providing income support, employment assistance, and mental health services.

Global Cooperation and Solidarity: The right to housing is a global issue that requires international cooperation and solidarity. As urbanization and globalization continue to shape housing markets and policies, there is a need for greater collaboration between governments, international organizations, and civil society to address housing inequalities and promote the right to housing on a global scale.

This may involve sharing best practices, providing technical assistance and funding to developing countries, and advocating for the inclusion of housing rights in global development agendas. Additionally, the international community must work together to address the root causes of displacement and housing insecurity, including conflict, climate change, and economic inequality.

Conclusion: Housing as a human right is a powerful concept that underscores the importance of safe, secure, and adequate shelter for the dignity and well-being of all individuals. While significant progress has been made in recognizing this right at the international level, its realization remains a challenge in many parts of the world. To address this challenge, governments and societies must commit to policies and practices that prioritize social equity, inclusion, and the protection of housing rights. By doing so, we can work towards a future where everyone has access to a home that meets their needs and supports their potential.

Food Security as a Human Right

Introduction

Food security, defined as the condition where all individuals have reliable access to sufficient, safe, and nutritious food to maintain a healthy and active life, is increasingly recognized as a fundamental human right. This right is enshrined in various international declarations and agreements, reflecting the global consensus that access to adequate food is essential for the dignity, well-being, and survival of every person. However, despite these commitments, food insecurity remains a pressing issue worldwide, affecting millions of people across different regions and socio-economic backgrounds. This analysis explores the concept of food security as a human right, its legal and ethical foundations, the challenges to its realization, and the potential pathways to achieving global food security.

1. The Concept and Legal Foundations of Food Security as a Human Right

Defining Food Security: Food security encompasses several key dimensions, including availability, access, utilization, and stability. Availability refers to the sufficient production of food; access involves the ability of individuals to obtain food through purchase, barter, or other means; utilization pertains to the proper use of food to meet dietary needs; and stability involves the consistent availability and access to food over time. Achieving food security requires addressing all these dimensions, ensuring that every individual has the necessary resources and opportunities to maintain a nutritious and balanced diet.

Legal Foundations: The recognition of food security as a human right is grounded in various international legal instruments. The Universal Declaration of Human Rights (UDHR), adopted by the United Nations General Assembly in 1948, explicitly mentions the right to adequate food in Article 25, stating that everyone has the right to a standard of living adequate for the health and well-being of themselves and their family, including food.

Further legal affirmation is found in the International Covenant on Economic, Social and Cultural Rights (ICESCR) of 1966, particularly in Article 11, which recognizes the "right of everyone to an adequate standard of living for themselves and their family, including adequate food, clothing, and housing, and to the continuous improvement of living conditions." The ICESCR also obligates states to take appropriate steps to ensure the realization of this right, including by improving methods of food production, conservation, and distribution.

Additionally, the 1996 World Food Summit in Rome and the subsequent Millennium Development Goals (MDGs) and Sustainable Development Goals (SDGs) have emphasized the global commitment to eradicating hunger and ensuring food security for all. The SDG 2, in particular, aims to "end hunger, achieve food security and improved nutrition, and promote sustainable agriculture" by 2030.

Ethical Foundations: The ethical foundation of food security as a human right is based on the principle of human dignity. Access to adequate food is essential for survival, health, and the ability to live a life of dignity and self-respect. Denying individuals the ability to meet their basic nutritional needs undermines their human dignity and violates their fundamental rights.

Furthermore, food security is closely linked to other human rights, such as the right to health, education, and work. Without adequate food, individuals cannot maintain their health, participate fully in education or employment, or contribute meaningfully to society. As such, ensuring food security is not only a moral obligation but also a necessary condition for the realization of a broader set of human rights.

2. Challenges to Realizing Food Security as a Human Right

Global Hunger and Malnutrition: Despite global progress in reducing hunger, significant challenges remain. According to the Food and Agriculture Organization (FAO), nearly 690 million people worldwide were undernourished in 2019, a number that has likely increased due to the impacts of the COVID-19 pandemic. Malnutrition, in the form of undernutrition, micronutrient deficiencies, and obesity, affects a large proportion of the global population, particularly in low- and middle-income countries.

The persistence of hunger and malnutrition is often rooted in complex socio-economic, political, and environmental factors. Poverty, inequality, conflict, and climate change are significant drivers of food insecurity, particularly in regions such as Sub-Saharan Africa, South Asia, and parts of Latin America. Addressing these underlying causes is crucial for realizing the right to food security.

Inequitable Food Systems: The global food system is characterized by significant inequalities in food production, distribution, and consumption. Large-scale industrial agriculture, driven by market forces, often prioritizes profit over the needs of local communities and the environment. This has led to the concentration of food production in the hands of a few multinational corporations, while smallholder farmers, who produce a significant portion of the world's food, struggle to access markets, resources, and fair prices for their products.

Moreover, the global trade system can exacerbate food insecurity by prioritizing exports over local food needs, leading to price volatility and food shortages in vulnerable regions. The commodification of food, coupled with speculative trading in food commodities, can result in price spikes that put essential foodstuffs out of reach for the poorest and most vulnerable populations.

Climate Change and Environmental Degradation: Climate change poses a significant threat to global food security, with rising temperatures, changing precipitation patterns, and more frequent extreme weather events disrupting agricultural production. Climate change disproportionately affects smallholder farmers and communities in developing countries, who are often least equipped to adapt to these changes.

Environmental degradation, including deforestation, soil erosion, and loss of biodiversity, further undermines food security by reducing the availability of arable land, decreasing crop yields, and disrupting ecosystems that are vital for food production. Sustainable agricultural practices and the protection of natural resources are essential for ensuring long-term food security.

Political and Economic Instability: Political instability, conflict, and economic crises are major contributors to food insecurity. In many regions, conflict disrupts food production and distribution, displaces populations, and exacerbates poverty and inequality. Economic crises, such as those caused by hyperinflation, currency devaluation, or economic sanctions, can lead to food shortages and make it difficult for people to afford basic necessities.

In such contexts, the right to food security is often violated, with vulnerable populations bearing the brunt of the impacts. International humanitarian assistance, peacebuilding efforts, and policies that promote economic stability and social protection are critical for addressing food insecurity in these situations.

3. Pathways to Achieving Global Food Security

Strengthening Local Food Systems: A key strategy for achieving food security is to strengthen local food systems that prioritize the needs of communities and promote sustainable agricultural practices. This involves supporting smallholder farmers, improving access to markets, and investing in infrastructure such as irrigation, storage facilities, and transportation networks. Local food systems that are resilient and self-sufficient are better equipped to withstand shocks, reduce dependence on external sources of food, and ensure that all members of the community have access to nutritious food.

Promoting Sustainable Agriculture: Sustainable agriculture is essential for ensuring long-term food security. This involves adopting farming practices that conserve natural resources, protect biodiversity, and reduce greenhouse gas emissions. Agroecology, organic farming, and regenerative agriculture are examples of sustainable approaches that can increase food production while preserving the environment.

Governments, international organizations, and civil society must work together to promote policies that support sustainable agriculture, including providing incentives for farmers to adopt environmentally friendly practices, investing in research and development, and implementing regulations that protect land, water, and other natural resources.

Ensuring Social Protection and Safety Nets: Social protection programs, such as food assistance, cash transfers, and school feeding programs, play a critical role in ensuring food security, particularly for vulnerable populations. These programs can help to mitigate the impacts of poverty, economic shocks, and natural disasters on food access and nutrition.

Governments should prioritize the expansion and strengthening of social protection systems to ensure that all individuals have access to adequate food, even in times of crisis. International cooperation and financing are also essential to support countries with limited resources in implementing effective social protection measures.

Addressing Inequality and Promoting Inclusive Growth: Addressing the root causes of inequality is crucial for achieving food security. This includes tackling issues such as land ownership, income disparities, and access to education and healthcare. Inclusive economic growth that provides opportunities for all members of society to participate in and benefit from the economy is essential for reducing poverty and ensuring food security.

Policies that promote fair wages, access to credit, and equal opportunities for women and marginalized groups can help to create a more equitable food system where everyone has the means to access nutritious food.

International Cooperation and Global Governance:
Achieving global food security requires international cooperation and effective global governance. This includes coordinating efforts to address climate change, managing global food trade, and providing humanitarian assistance in times of crisis. International organizations such as the United Nations, the World Food Programme (WFP), and the Food and Agriculture Organization (FAO) play a crucial role in facilitating cooperation and providing technical and financial support to countries in need.

Global governance structures must be reformed to ensure that they are inclusive, transparent, and accountable, with a focus on protecting the rights of the most vulnerable populations and promoting sustainable development.

Conclusion

Food security as a human right is a fundamental principle that underscores the importance of ensuring that all individuals have access to sufficient, safe, and nutritious food. While significant progress has been made in reducing hunger and improving food security, much work remains to be done to address the underlying causes of food insecurity, including poverty, inequality, environmental degradation, and political instability. Achieving global food security requires a comprehensive approach that includes strengthening local food systems, promoting sustainable agriculture, ensuring social protection, addressing inequality, and fostering international cooperation. By upholding the right to food security, societies can work towards a future where everyone has the opportunity to live a healthy and dignified life, free from hunger and malnutrition.

The Concept of Social Justice

Introduction

Social justice is a philosophical and political concept that seeks to ensure fair and equitable treatment of all individuals within a society. It encompasses a broad range of issues, including the distribution of wealth, opportunities, and privileges; the protection of human rights; and the elimination of systemic inequalities that marginalize specific groups. Social justice aims to create a society where all members can participate fully, without discrimination or bias, and where the benefits and burdens of society are distributed fairly. This analysis explores the origins, principles, and applications of social justice, its relevance in contemporary society, and the challenges and critiques it faces.

1. Origins and Foundations of Social Justice

Historical Context: The concept of social justice has its roots in ancient philosophical and religious traditions, where ideas about justice, fairness, and the common good were central to discussions about the organization of society. For example, in ancient Greece, philosophers like Plato and Aristotle explored the notion of justice as a virtue essential to the functioning of a well-ordered society. In religious traditions such as

Christianity, Islam, and Judaism, principles of charity, compassion, and equality are emphasized as moral imperatives that guide social relations.

However, the modern concept of social justice began to take shape in the 19th century, in response to the social and economic upheavals brought about by industrialization, urbanization, and the rise of capitalism. As inequalities in wealth and power became more pronounced, thinkers such as John Stuart Mill, Karl Marx, and John Rawls began to articulate theories of justice that emphasized the need for fair distribution of resources and opportunities.

Key Philosophical Foundations: Several key philosophical traditions have contributed to the development of social justice as a concept:

1. **Utilitarianism:** Utilitarianism, as articulated by thinkers like Jeremy Bentham and John Stuart Mill, holds that the best action is the one that maximizes overall happiness or well-being. In the context of social justice, utilitarian principles can be used to argue for policies and practices that reduce suffering and promote the greatest good for the greatest number. However, utilitarianism has also been criticized for

potentially justifying inequalities if they result in greater overall utility.

2. **Liberalism:** Liberal political philosophy, particularly as developed by John Locke and later by John Rawls, emphasizes individual rights, freedoms, and the rule of law. Rawls, in his seminal work "A Theory of Justice," introduced the idea of justice as fairness, which includes the principles of equal basic rights, equality of opportunity, and the difference principle, which permits social and economic inequalities only if they benefit the least advantaged members of society.

3. **Marxism:** Marxist theory offers a critique of capitalist societies, focusing on the ways in which economic inequalities and class structures lead to social injustice. Karl Marx argued that true social justice could only be achieved through the abolition of class distinctions and the establishment of a classless, communist society. While Marxist ideas have been influential, they have also been subject to criticism, particularly in relation to the authoritarian regimes that have claimed to implement Marxist principles.

4. **Feminist and Critical Theories:** Feminist theory and critical race theory have expanded the concept of social justice to include issues of

gender, race, and other forms of identity-based oppression. These theories highlight the ways in which social structures and cultural norms perpetuate inequalities and advocate for transformative changes to achieve greater equity and inclusion.

2. Principles and Applications of Social Justice

Key Principles of Social Justice: Social justice is built on several core principles that guide its application in various contexts:

1. **Equity:** Equity refers to the fair distribution of resources, opportunities, and treatment based on individual needs and circumstances. Unlike equality, which advocates for treating everyone the same, equity recognizes that different people have different needs and that achieving fairness requires addressing these differences.

2. **Access:** Social justice demands that all individuals have access to the resources and opportunities necessary to live a fulfilling life. This includes access to education, healthcare, employment, housing, and other basic needs, as well as opportunities for political and social participation.

3. **Participation:** A just society is one where all individuals have the opportunity to participate in the decision-making processes that affect their lives. This principle emphasizes the importance of democratic governance, inclusivity, and empowerment, particularly for marginalized and disenfranchised groups.

4. **Rights:** Social justice is closely linked to the protection and promotion of human rights. This includes civil and political rights, such as freedom of speech and the right to vote, as well as economic, social, and cultural rights, such as the right to work, education, and cultural expression.

5. **Fair Distribution:** Social justice seeks to ensure that the benefits and burdens of society are distributed fairly. This includes addressing economic inequalities, ensuring fair wages and working conditions, and promoting policies that reduce poverty and wealth disparities.

Applications in Contemporary Society: Social justice is applied across various domains, each with its own set of challenges and objectives:

1. **Economic Justice:** Economic justice is a central concern of social justice, focusing on issues such as income inequality, poverty, labor rights, and

fair taxation. Policies aimed at achieving economic justice may include progressive taxation, social safety nets, minimum wage laws, and efforts to reduce the wealth gap through wealth redistribution and access to opportunities.

2. **Racial and Ethnic Justice:** Racial and ethnic justice addresses the systemic discrimination and inequalities faced by people of color and ethnic minorities. This includes efforts to combat racism, promote affirmative action, and ensure equal treatment in areas such as education, employment, and criminal justice. Movements like Black Lives Matter have highlighted the ongoing struggle for racial justice in many societies.

3. **Gender Justice:** Gender justice seeks to address the inequalities and discrimination faced by individuals based on their gender or sexual orientation. Feminist movements have long advocated for gender justice, focusing on issues such as reproductive rights, gender-based violence, pay equity, and representation in political and social institutions.

4. **Environmental Justice:** Environmental justice links social justice with environmental issues, emphasizing the need to address the disproportionate impact of environmental

degradation and climate change on marginalized communities. This includes advocating for sustainable development, access to clean air and water, and policies that protect vulnerable populations from environmental harm.

5. **Health and Education:** Social justice extends to the realms of health and education, where it seeks to ensure that all individuals have access to quality healthcare and education, regardless of their socio-economic status. This includes addressing disparities in access to medical services, educational opportunities, and health outcomes, often through public policy and community-based initiatives.

3. Challenges and Critiques of Social Justice

Challenges in Implementation: While the principles of social justice are widely accepted, their implementation faces significant challenges. These include:

1. **Structural Inequalities:** Deep-rooted structural inequalities, such as those based on race, class, and gender, can be difficult to dismantle. These inequalities are often perpetuated by social institutions, cultural norms, and policies that favor certain groups over others.

2. **Political Resistance:** Efforts to promote social justice can encounter political resistance, particularly from those who benefit from the status quo. Policies aimed at redistributing wealth or expanding access to resources may be opposed by powerful interests, leading to conflicts and delays in implementation.

3. **Globalization and Neoliberalism:** The global economic system, characterized by neoliberal policies that prioritize market-driven growth and deregulation, often exacerbates social inequalities. Globalization can lead to a race to the bottom in labor standards, environmental protection, and social welfare, making it challenging to achieve social justice on a global scale.

4. **Resource Constraints:** Achieving social justice often requires significant resources, including financial investment, institutional support, and public engagement. In many cases, governments and organizations may lack the necessary resources to fully implement social justice initiatives, leading to gaps and inconsistencies in outcomes.

Critiques of Social Justice: Social justice has also faced criticism from various perspectives:

1. **Critiques from the Right:** Critics on the political right often argue that social justice initiatives lead to excessive government intervention, undermine individual responsibility, and stifle economic growth. They may also contend that efforts to achieve equity and inclusion can result in reverse discrimination or the erosion of merit-based systems.

2. **Critiques from the Left:** Some critics on the political left argue that mainstream approaches to social justice do not go far enough in addressing systemic inequalities. They may advocate for more radical changes, such as the abolition of capitalism, deeper redistributive policies, or the dismantling of oppressive institutions.

3. **Practicality and Effectiveness:** Some critiques focus on the practicality and effectiveness of social justice initiatives. Critics may argue that social justice policies are often difficult to implement, prone to unintended consequences, or insufficiently targeted to address the root causes of inequality.

Conclusion

Social justice is a complex and multifaceted concept that seeks to create a fair and equitable society where all individuals have the opportunity to thrive. Its

foundations in philosophy, law, and ethics underscore
its importance as a guiding principle for addressing the
inequalities and injustices that persist in contemporary
society. However, achieving social justice is fraught
with challenges, including structural inequalities,
political resistance, and resource constraints. Despite
these obstacles, the pursuit of social justice remains a
vital endeavor, offering a framework for creating a
more inclusive and just world where all people can
enjoy their rights and freedoms.

The Scientific Analysis of Human Genders

Introduction

The scientific study of human genders is a complex and evolving field that intersects biology, psychology, sociology, and anthropology. Traditionally, gender was often conflated with biological sex, leading to a binary understanding of human gender—male and female—based on physical and genetic characteristics. However, contemporary scientific research has increasingly recognized that gender is a multi-dimensional and fluid construct, encompassing a range of identities and expressions that go beyond the simple male-female dichotomy. This analysis explores the scientific understanding of gender, examining the biological, psychological, and social dimensions of gender, and how they interact to shape human identity.

1. Biological Foundations of Gender

Sex and Gender: Distinguishing the Terms: In scientific discourse, it is essential to distinguish between "sex" and "gender." Sex refers to the biological characteristics of an individual, including chromosomes, hormone levels, reproductive organs, and secondary sexual characteristics, which are typically categorized as male or female. Gender, on the other hand, refers to the roles, behaviors, activities, and

identities that a given society considers appropriate for
men, women, and other gender identities.

While sex is usually assigned at birth based on physical
anatomy, gender is a broader concept that encompasses
the social and psychological aspects of being male,
female, both, neither, or somewhere along the gender
spectrum. This distinction allows for a more nuanced
understanding of human diversity and acknowledges
that gender identity may not always align with
biological sex.

Chromosomal and Hormonal Influences:
Biologically, sex is determined by an individual's
chromosomes, with most humans having either XX
chromosomes (typically female) or XY chromosomes
(typically male). However, variations such as Turner
syndrome (X0), Klinefelter syndrome (XXY), and
androgen insensitivity syndrome demonstrate that sex is
not strictly binary. These variations, known as intersex
conditions, affect the development of sexual
characteristics and highlight the complexity of
biological sex.

Hormones also play a crucial role in the development of
gender-related characteristics. Testosterone, estrogen,
and other hormones influence the development of
primary and secondary sexual characteristics, such as

body hair, breast development, and voice pitch. However, hormonal influences on gender identity are not deterministic; they interact with a range of genetic, environmental, and social factors to shape individual gender identities.

Brain Structure and Gender Identity: Recent neuroscientific research has explored the relationship between brain structure and gender identity, investigating whether there are biological correlates to being male, female, or another gender. Some studies have found differences in certain brain regions, such as the hypothalamus, which are thought to be related to gender identity. For example, brain imaging studies have shown that transgender individuals may have brain structures that more closely align with their gender identity rather than their biological sex.

However, the interpretation of these findings is complex. The brain is highly plastic, meaning it can change and adapt throughout life in response to experiences and environmental factors. This plasticity suggests that while biology may play a role in gender identity, it is not the sole determinant. Additionally, the idea of a "male brain" or "female brain" has been criticized for reinforcing binary gender norms and overlooking the diversity of brain structures and functions that exist within all individuals.

2. Psychological and Social Dimensions of Gender

Gender Identity Development: Gender identity refers to an individual's deeply felt sense of being male, female, both, neither, or somewhere along the gender spectrum. This identity often develops early in childhood, typically between the ages of two and four, as children begin to recognize and express their gender identity. While many people identify with the gender they were assigned at birth (cisgender), others may identify with a different gender (transgender) or with multiple genders, or no gender at all (non-binary, genderqueer, or agender).

The development of gender identity is influenced by a combination of biological, psychological, and social factors. Psychologically, cognitive and emotional processes play a role in how individuals perceive and experience their gender. Socialization, or the process by which individuals learn and internalize the norms, roles, and behaviors associated with their culture's concept of gender, is also a significant factor. For example, the toys children are encouraged to play with, the clothes they are given, and the behaviors that are rewarded or discouraged all contribute to the formation of gender identity.

Gender Expression and Roles: Gender expression refers to how individuals present their gender to the outside world through clothing, behavior, speech, and other forms of self-presentation. Gender expression is distinct from gender identity; for example, a person with a male gender identity might express themselves in ways traditionally associated with femininity or vice versa.

Cultural norms and expectations heavily influence gender expression, but these norms can vary widely across different societies and historical periods. For instance, the color pink, now associated with femininity in many Western cultures, was once considered a masculine color. Similarly, gender roles—expectations about how individuals should behave based on their gender—are socially constructed and can differ significantly across cultures and eras.

The diversity of gender expressions and roles has led to a broader understanding of gender as a spectrum, rather than a binary. This perspective acknowledges that gender is not fixed or uniform but can change over time and vary from person to person.

Gender Dysphoria and Transgender Identity: Gender dysphoria is a psychological condition in which there is a significant disconnect between an individual's gender identity and the sex they were assigned at birth. This dissonance can lead to distress, anxiety, and a strong desire to live in a way that aligns with one's true gender identity. While not all transgender people experience gender dysphoria, it is a recognized condition in the Diagnostic and Statistical Manual of Mental Disorders (DSM-5).

The experiences of transgender individuals highlight the complex interaction between biology, identity, and society. Many transgender people undergo hormone therapy or gender-affirming surgeries to align their physical appearance with their gender identity. These medical interventions underscore the importance of recognizing and respecting diverse gender identities and the need for supportive health care that addresses the specific needs of transgender individuals.

3. Gender and Society: The Role of Culture and Social Norms

Cultural Variations in Gender: Gender is not a universal concept; it is shaped by cultural norms, traditions, and social structures. Anthropological studies have documented diverse gender identities and roles across different societies, challenging the idea that gender is naturally binary. For example, many Indigenous cultures in North America recognize Two-Spirit people, who embody both masculine and feminine qualities and are often seen as having a unique spiritual role within their communities.

Similarly, in South Asia, hijras are a recognized third gender, with a history that dates back centuries. These examples illustrate that gender is a social construct, with different cultures recognizing a variety of gender identities that go beyond the Western male-female binary.

Gender and Power Dynamics: Gender also intersects with power dynamics within society, influencing access to resources, opportunities, and rights. Feminist theory has long argued that gender roles and expectations are not merely social norms but are also mechanisms of control that maintain patriarchal systems of power. This perspective highlights the ways in which gender inequalities are perpetuated through social, political, and economic structures.

For instance, traditional gender roles have often relegated women to domestic spheres, limiting their access to education, employment, and political participation. Even in contemporary societies, gender disparities persist in areas such as income, career advancement, and representation in leadership positions. These inequalities are not solely the result of individual choices but are deeply rooted in historical and systemic biases that shape societal expectations and opportunities.

The Impact of Media and Technology: The media and technology also play a significant role in shaping and reinforcing gender norms. Media representations of gender often perpetuate stereotypes, depicting men and women in rigid, traditional roles. However, the rise of social media and digital platforms has also provided a space for challenging these norms and promoting more diverse and inclusive representations of gender.

Technology has also had a profound impact on gender identity and expression. The internet has facilitated the formation of online communities where individuals can explore and affirm their gender identities, access resources, and connect with others who share similar experiences. Additionally, advancements in medical technology, such as hormone replacement therapy and gender-affirming surgeries, have provided transgender individuals with more options for aligning their physical bodies with their gender identities.

4. Challenges and Future Directions in Gender Research

Addressing Bias and Expanding Research: Despite the progress made in understanding gender, scientific research has often been limited by biases that reflect societal norms. Historically, much of the research on gender has focused on binary, cisnormative frameworks, neglecting the experiences of transgender, non-binary, and intersex individuals. As a result, there is a need for more inclusive research that considers the full spectrum of gender identities and experiences.

Moreover, the study of gender must move beyond simplistic biological determinism and consider the complex interplay of genetics, hormones, environment, and culture. This requires interdisciplinary approaches that integrate insights from biology, psychology, sociology, and other fields to develop a more comprehensive understanding of gender.

Ethical Considerations and Human Rights: The scientific study of gender also raises important ethical considerations, particularly in relation to the treatment and rights of transgender and non-binary individuals. Researchers and healthcare providers must approach gender with sensitivity and respect, recognizing the diversity of gender identities and avoiding pathologizing or stigmatizing those who do not conform to traditional gender norms.

In addition, there is a growing recognition of the need to protect the human rights of individuals across the gender spectrum. This includes ensuring access to gender-affirming healthcare, legal recognition of gender identity, and protection from discrimination and violence. The fight for gender equality is not only a scientific issue but also a social justice imperative.

Conclusion

The scientific analysis of human genders reveals a complex and multifaceted reality that challenges traditional binary notions of male and female. Gender is influenced by a range of biological, psychological, and social factors, and it encompasses a spectrum of identities and expressions. As scientific understanding of gender continues to evolve, it is essential to adopt an inclusive and intersectional approach that respects the diversity of human experiences and promotes equality and justice for all individuals, regardless of their gender identity. The future of gender research holds the promise of greater understanding and acceptance, contributing to a more inclusive and equitable society.

The Scientific Analysis of Being Gay

Introduction

The scientific study of sexual orientation, including being gay, has evolved significantly over the past century. Historically, homosexuality was pathologized and misunderstood, but modern research has increasingly recognized that being gay is a natural variation of human sexuality. This analysis explores the biological, psychological, and social factors that contribute to sexual orientation, with a focus on the experiences of gay individuals. It also examines the societal implications of this research and the ongoing challenges in achieving full acceptance and equality for the LGBTQ+ community.

1. Biological Foundations of Sexual Orientation

Genetic Influences: Research into the genetic basis of sexual orientation has provided some evidence that genes play a role in determining whether someone is gay. Twin studies have shown that identical twins are more likely to share the same sexual orientation than fraternal twins, suggesting a genetic component. However, no single "gay gene" has been identified; instead, it is likely that multiple genes contribute to sexual orientation in complex ways.

A large-scale study published in 2019 analyzed the genomes of nearly half a million individuals and found that there are multiple genetic variants associated with same-sex sexual behavior, but these variants only account for a small proportion of the variability in sexual orientation. This indicates that while genetics are a factor, they are not the sole determinant of whether someone is gay. The study's findings emphasize the complexity of sexual orientation and suggest that it is influenced by a combination of genetic, environmental, and social factors.

Prenatal Hormonal Influences: Another area of research focuses on the role of prenatal hormones in shaping sexual orientation. The "fraternal birth order effect" is one of the most well-documented findings in this area. Studies have shown that men with older brothers are more likely to be gay, and the likelihood increases with the number of older brothers. This phenomenon is believed to be linked to the mother's immune response during pregnancy, which may affect the development of the male fetus's brain in ways that influence sexual orientation.

Hormonal theories suggest that exposure to different levels of sex hormones, such as testosterone and estrogen, in the womb may influence the development of sexual orientation. For example, some researchers hypothesize that lower levels of prenatal testosterone exposure may be associated with the development of a gay sexual orientation in males. However, these theories are still being studied, and the precise mechanisms by which prenatal hormones influence sexual orientation remain unclear.

Neuroanatomical Differences: Some studies have explored potential differences in brain structure between gay and heterosexual individuals. Research has found that certain regions of the brain, such as the hypothalamus, may differ in size or activity between gay and straight men. For example, a 1991 study by neuroscientist Simon LeVay found that a cluster of neurons in the hypothalamus was smaller in gay men compared to heterosexual men. LeVay's findings suggested a possible neurobiological basis for sexual orientation.

However, these studies are often limited by small sample sizes and methodological challenges, and their findings have been met with caution. While there may be neuroanatomical differences associated with sexual orientation, it is important to recognize that the brain is highly plastic and shaped by a wide range of biological, environmental, and social factors. Therefore, while neuroanatomical research provides intriguing insights, it is not definitive in explaining sexual orientation.

2. Psychological and Social Dimensions of Sexual Orientation

Development of Sexual Orientation: Sexual orientation is typically understood as a combination of sexual attraction, behavior, and identity. For gay individuals, this means experiencing romantic and sexual attraction to people of the same gender. The development of sexual orientation is thought to be a complex process influenced by a mix of genetic, hormonal, psychological, and social factors.

Most people become aware of their sexual orientation during adolescence, although some may recognize it earlier or later in life. The realization of being gay can be a deeply personal experience, often accompanied by a process of self-acceptance. For many, this process is influenced by societal attitudes toward homosexuality, which can range from acceptance and support to stigma and discrimination.

Sexual Orientation and Mental Health: Research has shown that sexual orientation itself is not a mental health disorder. However, the experience of being gay in a society that may stigmatize or discriminate against LGBTQ+ individuals can impact mental health. Studies have consistently found that gay individuals are at a higher risk for mental health challenges, including anxiety, depression, and suicide, compared to their heterosexual peers. This increased risk is largely attributed to the stress of navigating a world that may be hostile or unaccepting of their sexual orientation.

The concept of "minority stress" is often used to explain the mental health disparities observed in gay and other sexual minority populations. Minority stress refers to the chronic stress that results from societal stigma, prejudice, and discrimination. This stress can manifest in various ways, including internalized homophobia, where individuals absorb negative societal attitudes toward homosexuality and apply them to themselves.

Social Support and Community: Despite the challenges, social support and community can play a crucial role in the well-being of gay individuals. LGBTQ+ communities provide spaces where individuals can find acceptance, support, and validation. These communities often serve as important sources of social connection, identity affirmation, and resilience in the face of societal discrimination.

Research has shown that strong social support networks, including supportive family and friends, are protective factors against the negative mental health outcomes associated with minority stress. Positive relationships and community involvement can help mitigate the impact of discrimination and foster a sense of belonging and self-worth.

3. The Societal Context of Being Gay

Historical and Cultural Perspectives: The societal understanding and acceptance of homosexuality have varied greatly across different cultures and historical periods. In some ancient civilizations, such as Greece and Rome, same-sex relationships were relatively accepted, particularly among men. However, in many other societies, homosexuality has been stigmatized, criminalized, or pathologized.

In the Western world, the 19th and 20th centuries saw homosexuality classified as a mental disorder, with efforts to "cure" gay individuals through various forms of conversion therapy. It was not until 1973 that the American Psychiatric Association removed homosexuality from the Diagnostic and Statistical Manual of Mental Disorders (DSM), a significant milestone in the path toward de-stigmatization.

Today, societal attitudes toward homosexuality vary widely. In many parts of the world, being gay is increasingly accepted, with legal protections against discrimination and the recognition of same-sex marriages. However, in other regions, homosexuality remains illegal and heavily stigmatized, with gay individuals facing severe legal penalties, social ostracism, and violence.

The Role of Social Movements: The advancement of gay rights has been largely driven by social movements that advocate for the acceptance, equality, and legal protection of LGBTQ+ individuals. The Stonewall Riots of 1969, often cited as the catalyst for the modern LGBTQ+ rights movement, marked a turning point in the fight against discrimination. Since then, activists have worked tirelessly to secure rights for gay individuals, including the decriminalization of homosexuality, the legalization of same-sex marriage, and protections against discrimination in employment, housing, and public accommodations.

These movements have also played a crucial role in challenging harmful stereotypes and promoting a more inclusive understanding of sexual orientation. Through education, advocacy, and visibility, LGBTQ+ rights organizations have helped shift public attitudes and foster greater acceptance of diverse sexual orientations.

Current Challenges and Future Directions: Despite significant progress, gay individuals continue to face challenges, including discrimination, violence, and legal inequalities, particularly in regions where LGBTQ+ rights are not fully recognized. Moreover, the rise of anti-LGBTQ+ rhetoric and policies in some areas poses ongoing threats to the well-being and rights of gay individuals.

Moving forward, continued research is needed to better understand the experiences and needs of gay individuals, particularly in areas such as mental health, healthcare access, and social support. Efforts to combat discrimination and promote acceptance must also continue, both at the societal level and within specific communities and institutions.

Conclusion

The scientific analysis of being gay reveals a complex interplay of biological, psychological, and social factors that shape sexual orientation. While genetics and prenatal influences play a role, sexual orientation is not determined by any single factor but rather emerges from a combination of influences. The experience of being gay is also shaped by societal attitudes, which can either support or challenge an individual's well-being. As society continues to evolve, it is essential to build on the progress made toward understanding and accepting sexual diversity, ensuring that all individuals, regardless of their sexual orientation, can live free from discrimination and with full recognition of their rights.

The LGBTQ+ Movement: History, Progress, and Ongoing Struggles

Introduction

The LGBTQ+ movement is one of the most significant social justice movements of the modern era, advocating for the rights and recognition of individuals who identify as lesbian, gay, bisexual, transgender, queer, and other non-heteronormative identities. Over the past century, the movement has made remarkable strides in challenging discriminatory laws, shifting societal attitudes, and securing legal protections for LGBTQ+ individuals. However, the struggle for equality and acceptance continues, as many in the community still face discrimination, violence, and systemic barriers. This analysis explores the history, achievements, challenges, and future directions of the LGBTQ+ movement.

1. Historical Overview of the LGBTQ+ Movement

Early Beginnings: The roots of the LGBTQ+ movement can be traced back to the late 19th and early 20th centuries, when the first organized efforts to advocate for homosexual rights began to emerge in Europe and the United States. In Germany, the Scientific-Humanitarian Committee, founded by Magnus Hirschfeld in 1897, was one of the first organizations dedicated to advocating for the decriminalization of homosexuality and promoting scientific research on sexual orientation.

In the United States, the 1920s and 1930s saw the emergence of small but significant groups that advocated for homosexual rights, such as the Society for Human Rights in Chicago, founded in 1924. However, these early efforts were met with strong resistance, and the movement struggled to gain traction in a society that largely viewed homosexuality as immoral or criminal.

The Mid-20th Century: The Homophile Movement: The mid-20th century marked the rise of the homophile movement, which sought to promote the rights of homosexual individuals through more moderate and assimilationist tactics. Organizations like the Mattachine Society, founded in 1950 by Harry Hay, and the Daughters of Bilitis, founded in 1955 by Del Martin and Phyllis Lyon, worked to create safe spaces for gay men and lesbians and to advocate for their rights in a society that was deeply hostile to them.

The homophile movement emphasized respectability and sought to demonstrate that homosexuals were no different from their heterosexual counterparts, except in their sexual orientation. This approach, while criticized by some for being too conservative, laid the groundwork for future activism by creating a visible, organized community that could advocate for change.

The Stonewall Riots and the Birth of the Modern LGBTQ+ Movement: The modern LGBTQ+ movement is often traced back to the Stonewall Riots, which took place in New York City in June 1969. The riots began when patrons of the Stonewall Inn, a gay bar in Greenwich Village, resisted a police raid—a common occurrence at the time, as law enforcement frequently targeted LGBTQ+ spaces. The spontaneous uprising that followed marked a turning point in the fight for LGBTQ+ rights.

The Stonewall Riots galvanized the LGBTQ+ community, leading to the formation of more militant and visible organizations, such as the Gay Liberation Front (GLF) and the Gay Activists Alliance (GAA). These groups rejected the assimilationist approach of the homophile movement and instead embraced a more radical, confrontational stance, demanding immediate and widespread change.

The first anniversary of the Stonewall Riots was commemorated with the first Pride marches in New York City, Los Angeles, and Chicago, marking the beginning of an annual tradition that would spread across the world. Pride events became a powerful symbol of LGBTQ+ visibility, resistance, and solidarity, celebrating the diversity of the community and demanding recognition and rights.

2. Achievements of the LGBTQ+ Movement

Legal and Political Victories: One of the most significant achievements of the LGBTQ+ movement has been the decriminalization of homosexuality. In the United States, the Supreme Court's landmark 2003 decision in *Lawrence v. Texas* struck down sodomy laws nationwide, effectively decriminalizing consensual same-sex sexual activity. This ruling was a critical victory in the fight for LGBTQ+ rights, overturning centuries of legal discrimination.

The movement has also made significant strides in securing legal recognition for same-sex relationships. In 2015, the U.S. Supreme Court's decision in *Obergefell v. Hodges* legalized same-sex marriage nationwide, marking a major milestone in the fight for marriage equality. This victory was the culmination of decades of activism and legal battles, beginning with the first legal challenges to same-sex marriage bans in the 1970s.

In addition to marriage equality, the LGBTQ+ movement has successfully advocated for protections against discrimination in employment, housing, and public accommodations. For example, in 2020, the U.S. Supreme Court ruled in *Bostock v. Clayton County* that Title VII of the Civil Rights Act of 1964, which prohibits employment discrimination based on sex, also applies to discrimination based on sexual orientation and gender identity. This decision extended crucial legal protections to millions of LGBTQ+ workers.

Advances in Transgender Rights: The LGBTQ+ movement has also made significant progress in advancing the rights of transgender individuals, who have historically been marginalized within both the broader society and the LGBTQ+ community. Activism by transgender individuals and allies has led to greater visibility and recognition of transgender identities, as well as legal protections against discrimination.

In recent years, there has been increased focus on issues such as access to gender-affirming healthcare, the right to update legal documents to reflect one's gender identity, and the fight against discriminatory policies, such as bans on transgender individuals serving in the military. The transgender rights movement has also challenged societal norms around gender, promoting a more inclusive understanding of gender diversity.

Cultural and Social Impact: Beyond legal and political victories, the LGBTQ+ movement has had a profound impact on culture and society. LGBTQ+ representation in media, literature, and art has increased dramatically over the past few decades, helping to shift public perceptions and challenge stereotypes. This visibility has played a crucial role in fostering greater acceptance and understanding of LGBTQ+ individuals.

Pride events, which began as acts of resistance and defiance, have evolved into global celebrations of LGBTQ+ identity and culture. These events provide an opportunity for LGBTQ+ individuals to express themselves freely, connect with their community, and advocate for continued progress. Pride has become a powerful symbol of resilience, joy, and the ongoing fight for equality.

3. Ongoing Challenges and Future Directions

Continued Discrimination and Violence: Despite the progress made, LGBTQ+ individuals continue to face significant challenges. Discrimination, harassment, and violence remain pervasive issues, particularly for transgender individuals, LGBTQ+ people of color, and those living in regions where LGBTQ+ rights are not fully recognized. Hate crimes against LGBTQ+ individuals, including acts of violence and murder, are still a serious concern, and many LGBTQ+ people experience discrimination in areas such as healthcare, housing, and education.

The rise of anti-LGBTQ+ rhetoric and policies in some parts of the world, including efforts to roll back legal protections and restrict LGBTQ+ rights, underscores the fragility of the progress that has been made. In some countries, homosexuality is still criminalized, and LGBTQ+ individuals face severe legal penalties, social ostracism, and even death.

Intersectionality and Inclusivity: As the LGBTQ+ movement continues to evolve, there is an increasing focus on the importance of intersectionality—recognizing that individuals experience discrimination and oppression in multiple, interconnected ways. This includes understanding how factors such as race, gender, class, and disability intersect with sexual orientation and gender identity to shape the experiences of LGBTQ+ individuals.

There is also a growing recognition of the need for greater inclusivity within the LGBTQ+ movement itself. Historically, the movement has often been dominated by the concerns of white, cisgender, middle-class gay men, with the needs and voices of other groups, such as transgender people, people of color, and those from lower socioeconomic backgrounds, being marginalized. Ensuring that the movement is truly inclusive and representative of all LGBTQ+ individuals is a key challenge moving forward.

Global LGBTQ+ Rights: While significant progress has been made in many countries, the fight for LGBTQ+ rights is far from over on a global scale. In many parts of the world, LGBTQ+ individuals continue to face severe repression, and the movement must address the ongoing human rights abuses against LGBTQ+ people in these regions. International solidarity and advocacy are essential in pushing for global recognition of LGBTQ+ rights as human rights.

Conclusion

The LGBTQ+ movement has achieved remarkable progress in advancing the rights and recognition of LGBTQ+ individuals, transforming societal attitudes and securing legal protections that were once unimaginable. However, the movement's work is not finished. Ongoing challenges, including discrimination, violence, and the need for greater inclusivity and intersectionality, require continued activism and advocacy. As the movement looks to the future, it must remain vigilant in protecting the gains that have been made while pushing for a world where all LGBTQ+ individuals can live with dignity, equality, and respect.

The fight for LGBTQ+ rights is not just a struggle for one community; it is a broader struggle for human rights, justice, and equality for all.

The Pro-Choice Movement: Advocacy, Achievements, and Challenges

Introduction

The pro-choice movement is a critical component of the broader struggle for reproductive rights, centered on the belief that individuals should have the autonomy to make decisions about their own bodies, including the right to access safe and legal abortion. This movement has been at the forefront of some of the most heated and enduring debates in modern history, particularly in the United States. Over the decades, the pro-choice movement has achieved significant legal victories, challenged restrictive laws, and worked to ensure that reproductive healthcare is accessible to all. However, it continues to face formidable opposition and challenges as it advocates for reproductive justice.

1. The Origins and Evolution of the Pro-Choice Movement

Early Struggles for Reproductive Rights: The roots of the pro-choice movement can be traced back to the early 20th century when advocates for women's rights began to challenge restrictive laws that criminalized abortion and limited access to contraception. Pioneers like Margaret Sanger, who founded the American Birth Control League (which later became Planned Parenthood), were instrumental in advocating for the right of women to access birth control and make decisions about their reproductive health.

During the early 20th century, abortion was illegal in most parts of the United States, and women who sought abortions often faced dangerous, clandestine procedures that put their health and lives at risk. The pro-choice movement emerged as part of the broader women's rights movement, advocating for the decriminalization of abortion and the right to choose as essential components of gender equality.

The Legalization of Abortion: Roe v. Wade and Its Impact: The landmark U.S. Supreme Court decision in *Roe v. Wade* in 1973 was a pivotal moment in the history of the pro-choice movement. The Court ruled that the constitutional right to privacy extended to a woman's decision to have an abortion, effectively legalizing abortion nationwide. This decision was based on the understanding that the government should not interfere with a woman's right to make decisions about her own body.

Roe v. Wade was a significant victory for the pro-choice movement, as it recognized a woman's right to choose abortion within certain limits and established a framework for regulating abortion based on the trimester of pregnancy. This decision not only made abortion safer and more accessible for millions of women but also energized the pro-choice movement, which became a powerful force in advocating for reproductive rights.

In the years following *Roe v. Wade*, the pro-choice movement expanded its focus to include broader issues of reproductive justice, advocating for access to contraception, comprehensive sex education, and affordable reproductive healthcare. The movement also worked to protect and expand the rights established by *Roe v. Wade*, challenging state and federal laws that sought to restrict access to abortion and undermine reproductive rights.

Challenges and Backlash: Despite the success of *Roe v. Wade*, the pro-choice movement has faced ongoing challenges and backlash from anti-abortion activists and lawmakers. In the years following the decision, a well-organized and determined anti-abortion movement emerged, seeking to overturn *Roe* and impose stricter regulations on abortion. This led to a series of legal battles and state-level restrictions aimed at limiting access to abortion.

One of the most significant challenges came in the form of the 1992 Supreme Court case *Planned Parenthood v. Casey*, which upheld the core principle of *Roe v. Wade* but allowed for increased regulation of abortion, as long as those regulations did not place an "undue burden" on a woman's ability to obtain an abortion. This ruling opened the door for states to pass a variety of restrictive laws, such as mandatory waiting periods, parental consent requirements, and targeted regulation of abortion providers (TRAP laws).

These restrictions have had a profound impact on access to abortion, particularly for low-income women, women of color, and those living in rural areas. The pro-choice movement has worked tirelessly to challenge these laws in court and advocate for the repeal of restrictive measures, but the ongoing erosion of abortion rights has remained a significant concern.

2. The Pro-Choice Movement Today

Reproductive Justice and Intersectionality: In recent years, the pro-choice movement has increasingly embraced the concept of reproductive justice, which was first articulated by women of color in the 1990s. Reproductive justice expands the focus beyond the legal right to abortion and emphasizes the need for a comprehensive approach to reproductive rights that addresses the social, economic, and racial inequalities that affect access to reproductive healthcare.

Reproductive justice advocates argue that the right to choose an abortion is meaningless if individuals do not have access to the necessary resources, such as affordable healthcare, childcare, and economic opportunities, to make meaningful choices about their reproductive lives. The movement calls for a broader understanding of reproductive rights that includes the right to have children, the right not to have children, and the right to parent children in safe and healthy environments.

This intersectional approach has broadened the pro-choice movement's goals and strategies, making it more inclusive and responsive to the diverse needs of different communities. It has also led to stronger alliances between the pro-choice movement and other social justice movements, including those focused on racial justice, economic justice, and LGBTQ+ rights.

The Role of Advocacy and Activism: Advocacy and activism remain central to the pro-choice movement's efforts to protect and expand reproductive rights. Organizations such as Planned Parenthood, NARAL Pro-Choice America, and the Center for Reproductive Rights play a crucial role in providing reproductive healthcare, defending abortion rights in court, and lobbying for pro-choice policies at the state and federal levels.

Grassroots activism has also been a powerful force in the pro-choice movement. Local activists and organizations work to raise awareness, provide support to individuals seeking abortions, and mobilize communities to resist restrictive laws. The rise of digital activism and social media has enabled the pro-choice movement to reach wider audiences, organize large-scale protests, and amplify the voices of those most affected by abortion restrictions.

One of the most notable recent examples of pro-choice activism was the response to the passage of highly restrictive abortion laws in states such as Texas and Alabama in 2019. These laws, which effectively banned most abortions and threatened providers with severe penalties, sparked widespread outrage and mobilized a national movement to protect reproductive rights. Pro-choice activists organized rallies, filed legal challenges, and launched campaigns to support abortion providers and patients in affected states.

Challenges and the Future of the Pro-Choice Movement: The pro-choice movement continues to face significant challenges, particularly in the wake of the U.S. Supreme Court's 2022 decision in *Dobbs v. Jackson Women's Health Organization*, which overturned *Roe v. Wade* and eliminated the federal constitutional right to abortion. This decision returned the authority to regulate abortion to individual states, leading to a patchwork of laws across the country, with some states enacting total bans and others protecting or expanding abortion access.

In the post-*Dobbs* era, the pro-choice movement is focused on several key areas: defending abortion access in states where it remains legal, challenging restrictive laws in court, supporting individuals who need to travel to obtain abortions, and advocating for federal legislation to protect reproductive rights. The movement is also working to address the broader social and economic barriers that limit access to reproductive healthcare and to ensure that reproductive justice is a central component of broader social justice efforts.

As the pro-choice movement looks to the future, it faces the dual challenge of resisting further erosion of reproductive rights while also building a more inclusive and intersectional movement that addresses the full range of issues affecting reproductive autonomy. This includes continuing to advocate for the right to safe and legal abortion while also addressing the broader social and economic conditions that impact individuals' ability to make choices about their reproductive lives,

Conclusion

The pro-choice movement has been a powerful force for advancing reproductive rights and gender equality over the past century. Through legal victories, grassroots activism, and advocacy for reproductive justice, the movement has fought to ensure that individuals have the autonomy to make decisions about their own bodies. However, the struggle for reproductive rights is far from over, particularly in the wake of recent legal setbacks. The pro-choice movement must continue to adapt and respond to new challenges, working to protect and expand reproductive rights in an increasingly complex and divided landscape. As the movement evolves, it remains committed to the principle that reproductive rights are fundamental human rights, essential to achieving true gender equality and social justice.

The Current Status of American Immigration

Introduction

Immigration has long been a central issue in American politics, shaping the nation's demographics, economy, and cultural landscape. The current status of American immigration is marked by a complex interplay of policies, public opinion, and global events. In recent years, immigration policy has been a focal point of political debate, with significant shifts occurring under different administrations. This analysis explores the current state of American immigration, examining the policies in place, the challenges faced by immigrants, and the broader implications for society.

1. Immigration Policy and Enforcement

Policy Shifts and Legislative Landscape: The U.S. immigration system has undergone substantial changes in recent years, particularly in response to differing political ideologies. Under the Trump administration (2017–2021), immigration policy saw a marked shift towards stricter enforcement and reduced legal immigration pathways. Policies such as the "zero-tolerance" policy, which led to family separations at the border, the travel ban targeting several predominantly Muslim countries, and efforts to end the Deferred

Action for Childhood Arrivals (DACA) program, highlighted a more restrictive approach to immigration.

The Biden administration has sought to reverse many of these policies, emphasizing a more humane and inclusive approach to immigration. However, despite efforts to undo some of the previous administration's policies, the Biden administration has faced significant challenges in implementing comprehensive immigration reform. Legislative gridlock in Congress has stalled efforts to pass significant reforms, leaving many aspects of the immigration system in limbo.

One of the key areas of focus has been on providing a pathway to citizenship for undocumented immigrants, particularly those who arrived in the U.S. as children (often referred to as "Dreamers") and recipients of Temporary Protected Status (TPS). While there have been legislative proposals to address these issues, including the American Dream and Promise Act, none have yet been enacted into law.

Border Security and Asylum Policy: Border security remains a contentious issue in the U.S. immigration debate. The southern border with Mexico has been a focal point, with varying approaches to managing migration flows. The Trump administration's focus on building a border wall and implementing policies like the Migrant Protection Protocols (MPP), also known as the "Remain in Mexico" policy, aimed to deter illegal immigration and asylum seekers. These policies faced significant legal and humanitarian challenges.

The Biden administration has taken steps to dismantle some of these measures, but the situation at the border remains complex. The administration ended the MPP program, allowing asylum seekers to wait for their U.S. immigration court hearings within the U.S. rather than in Mexico. However, the influx of migrants at the border, driven by factors such as violence, poverty, and climate change in Central America, has strained the immigration system.

In response, the Biden administration has faced criticism from both sides of the political spectrum—conservatives argue that the administration's policies have encouraged more illegal immigration, while progressives contend that the administration has not done enough to address the humanitarian needs of migrants. The administration has also reintroduced policies like Title 42, which allows for the rapid expulsion of migrants at the border under the guise of public health concerns during the COVID-19 pandemic. This policy has been controversial, with critics arguing that it violates the rights of asylum seekers.

Refugee Admissions and Global Crises: The U.S. refugee admissions program has also seen significant changes in recent years. Under the Trump administration, refugee admissions were drastically reduced, reaching historically low levels. The Biden administration initially faced criticism for maintaining low refugee admission caps, but later raised the cap, signaling a commitment to rebuilding the refugee resettlement program.

Global crises, such as the conflict in Afghanistan, the war in Ukraine, and instability in various parts of the world, have increased the demand for refugee resettlement. The U.S. has responded by admitting thousands of Afghan refugees following the U.S. withdrawal from Afghanistan in 2021 and by providing Temporary Protected Status (TPS) to Ukrainian nationals in response to the Russian invasion of Ukraine.

However, the U.S. refugee resettlement system continues to face challenges, including bureaucratic delays, limited resources, and the need for more robust infrastructure to support the resettlement and integration of refugees. The ongoing global displacement crisis underscores the importance of a responsive and humane refugee policy.

2. Challenges Faced by Immigrants

Legal and Undocumented Immigrants: Immigrants in the U.S., whether documented or undocumented, face a range of challenges. For undocumented immigrants, the lack of legal status creates significant barriers to accessing basic services, employment opportunities, and legal protections. Many live in fear of deportation and separation from their families. While DACA has provided temporary relief to some undocumented immigrants, the uncertainty surrounding the program's future remains a significant source of anxiety.

Even legal immigrants face obstacles, including long wait times for family reunification visas, challenges in navigating the complex immigration system, and discrimination in the labor market. The COVID-19 pandemic has exacerbated these challenges, with immigrants disproportionately affected by job losses, health risks, and barriers to accessing healthcare and economic relief programs.

Integration and Social Challenges: The integration of immigrants into American society remains a critical issue. Language barriers, cultural differences, and the lack of access to quality education and employment opportunities can hinder the successful integration of immigrants. Anti-immigrant sentiment and xenophobia further exacerbate these challenges, leading to discrimination and social exclusion.

The rise of anti-immigrant rhetoric in political discourse has had a tangible impact on the experiences of immigrants in the U.S. Hate crimes against immigrants, particularly those perceived as being of Latino or Muslim background, have increased in recent years. This hostile environment can create a sense of alienation and fear among immigrant communities, making it more difficult for them to fully participate in American society.

Efforts to promote integration have included initiatives to improve language access, provide legal services, and support immigrant entrepreneurship. Community-based organizations and advocacy groups play a vital role in helping immigrants navigate these challenges and advocating for policies that promote inclusion and equity.

3. Broader Implications and Future Outlook

Economic Impact of Immigration: Immigration has a significant impact on the U.S. economy, contributing to labor force growth, innovation, and cultural diversity. Immigrants make up a substantial portion of the workforce in key industries, such as agriculture, construction, healthcare, and technology. They also contribute to economic growth through entrepreneurship, with immigrant-owned businesses playing a vital role in local and national economies.

However, the debate over the economic impact of immigration remains polarized. Proponents argue that immigrants fill critical labor shortages, drive innovation, and contribute to the tax base. Opponents, on the other hand, often raise concerns about competition for jobs, wage suppression, and the strain on public services.

The future of immigration policy will likely have significant implications for the U.S. economy. Policies that promote legal pathways for immigration, protect the rights of workers, and support the integration of immigrants into the workforce are essential for ensuring that immigration continues to be a positive force for economic growth.

Political and Social Implications: The political landscape surrounding immigration is deeply divided, with immigration policy often serving as a flashpoint in national elections and public discourse. The polarization of the immigration debate has made it difficult to achieve bipartisan consensus on comprehensive immigration reform, leading to a piecemeal approach that often fails to address the root causes of migration or the needs of immigrants.

The ongoing debate over immigration also has broader social implications, shaping public attitudes toward diversity, inclusion, and national identity. The way in which immigration is framed in public discourse can influence how immigrants are perceived and treated in society. Efforts to foster a more inclusive and equitable approach to immigration will require addressing these underlying social dynamics and promoting a narrative that recognizes the contributions and humanity of immigrants.

Conclusion

The current status of American immigration is characterized by significant challenges and ongoing debates. While there have been efforts to create a more humane and inclusive immigration system, political polarization, legal obstacles, and social challenges continue to impede progress. The future of American immigration will depend on the ability of policymakers, advocates, and communities to navigate these complexities and work towards a system that upholds the rights and dignity of all immigrants. As the U.S. grapples with the realities of a changing global landscape, immigration will remain a critical issue with far-reaching implications for the nation's future.

Introduction

Environmental activism is a powerful and dynamic movement that seeks to protect the planet from the detrimental impacts of human activities. This form of activism encompasses a wide range of activities, from grassroots organizing to global advocacy, aimed at addressing environmental challenges such as climate change, pollution, deforestation, and biodiversity loss. Over the past several decades, environmental activists have played a crucial role in raising awareness, influencing policy, and driving societal change toward more sustainable practices. This analysis explores the evolution of environmental activism, its key strategies and achievements, and the ongoing challenges it faces.

1. The Evolution of Environmental Activism

Early Roots and the Rise of Modern Environmentalism: The origins of environmental activism can be traced back to the conservation movements of the late 19th and early 20th centuries, which focused on preserving natural landscapes and wildlife. Figures like John Muir and Theodore Roosevelt were instrumental in advocating for the establishment of national parks and protected areas in the United States. These early efforts laid the groundwork for a broader environmental consciousness that would emerge in the following decades.

The modern environmental movement began to take shape in the 1960s and 1970s, fueled by growing concerns about industrial pollution, resource depletion, and the impacts of human activity on the natural world. The publication of Rachel Carson's seminal book *Silent Spring* in 1962 is often credited with igniting the environmental movement. Carson's work highlighted the dangers of pesticide use, particularly DDT, and its devastating effects on wildlife and ecosystems. *Silent Spring* galvanized public awareness and led to a wave of environmental activism focused on addressing pollution and protecting natural resources.

The first Earth Day, celebrated on April 22, 1970, marked a significant milestone in the environmental movement, bringing together millions of people across the United States to demand action on environmental issues. The success of Earth Day helped to establish environmentalism as a major social and political force, leading to the creation of the Environmental Protection Agency (EPA) and the passage of landmark environmental legislation, including the Clean Air Act, Clean Water Act, and Endangered Species Act.

Environmental Justice and Global Activism: As the environmental movement evolved, it increasingly recognized the intersection of environmental issues with social justice concerns. The environmental justice movement, which emerged in the 1980s, highlighted the disproportionate impact of environmental hazards on marginalized communities, particularly communities of color and low-income populations. Activists within this movement sought to address issues such as toxic waste disposal, air and water pollution, and lack of access to clean and safe environments in these communities.

Global environmental activism has also gained prominence, particularly in response to the growing awareness of climate change. International environmental organizations, such as Greenpeace, the World Wildlife Fund (WWF), and Friends of the Earth, have been at the forefront of campaigns to protect the environment and advocate for sustainable development. These organizations have played a key role in shaping global environmental policy, influencing international agreements such as the Kyoto Protocol and the Paris Agreement.

The rise of global environmental activism has also been facilitated by the spread of digital communication technologies, which have enabled activists to mobilize supporters, share information, and coordinate actions across borders. Social media platforms have become powerful tools for raising awareness about environmental issues, organizing protests, and pressuring governments and corporations to take action.

2. Strategies and Achievements of Environmental Activism

Grassroots Organizing and Direct Action: Grassroots organizing has been a cornerstone of environmental activism, empowering local communities to take action on environmental issues that directly affect them. Grassroots activists often work to protect local ecosystems, advocate for sustainable land use, and resist environmentally harmful development projects. This form of activism is characterized by community involvement, direct action, and the use of innovative tactics to draw attention to environmental concerns.

One notable example of grassroots environmental activism is the Standing Rock Sioux Tribe's resistance to the Dakota Access Pipeline (DAPL) in 2016. The tribe, along with environmental activists and allies from across the country, protested the construction of the pipeline, which they argued threatened their water supply and violated sacred lands. The movement garnered widespread national and international support, highlighting the connections between environmental protection and Indigenous rights.

Direct action, such as protests, sit-ins, and blockades, has been a key tactic of environmental activists seeking to disrupt environmentally harmful activities and draw public attention to their causes. Organizations like Extinction Rebellion and Greenpeace are known for their use of nonviolent direct action to confront governments and corporations over their environmental policies and practices. These actions often involve high-profile demonstrations designed to create a sense of urgency and demand immediate action on environmental issues.

Policy Advocacy and Legal Action: Environmental activism has also been highly effective in influencing public policy and shaping environmental regulations. Activists and environmental organizations work to advocate for stronger environmental laws, hold policymakers accountable, and ensure the enforcement of existing regulations. This advocacy often involves lobbying, public campaigns, and engagement with the legislative process.

Legal action is another critical tool used by environmental activists to protect the environment and hold polluters accountable. Environmental organizations frequently engage in litigation to challenge harmful activities, enforce environmental laws, and secure protections for endangered species and ecosystems. Landmark legal cases, such as Massachusetts v. EPA, which established the EPA's authority to regulate greenhouse gas emissions, have had significant impacts on environmental policy in the United States.

Corporate Accountability and Consumer Activism: In recent years, environmental activists have increasingly focused on holding corporations accountable for their environmental impact. This includes campaigns to pressure companies to reduce their carbon footprint, eliminate plastic waste, and adopt sustainable practices. Activists often use shareholder activism, consumer boycotts, and public campaigns to influence corporate behavior.

The divestment movement, which encourages institutions and individuals to withdraw investments from fossil fuel companies, has gained significant momentum as a strategy to combat climate change. By targeting the financial sector, divestment activists aim to shift capital away from environmentally harmful industries and towards renewable energy and sustainable development.

Consumer activism, which involves using purchasing power to support environmentally responsible products and companies, has also become an important aspect of environmental activism. The rise of eco-conscious consumers has led to increased demand for sustainable products, influencing corporate practices and driving market trends towards greater environmental responsibility.

3. Challenges and the Future of Environmental Activism

Climate Change and Global Environmental Challenges: Climate change is arguably the most pressing environmental issue of our time, posing an existential threat to ecosystems, economies, and human societies. Addressing climate change requires coordinated global action and a fundamental transformation of energy systems, consumption patterns, and economic practices. Environmental activists have been at the forefront of efforts to raise awareness about the urgency of climate action and to advocate for policies that reduce greenhouse gas emissions and promote renewable energy.

However, the scale and complexity of the climate crisis present significant challenges for environmental activists. The entrenched interests of the fossil fuel industry, political resistance, and the slow pace of international negotiations have made it difficult to achieve the necessary level of action to mitigate climate change. Activists continue to push for more ambitious climate policies, but the window for avoiding the worst impacts of climate change is rapidly closing.

Environmental Activism in the Digital Age: The digital age has transformed the landscape of environmental activism, providing new tools for organizing, communication, and advocacy. Social media platforms, online petitions, and crowdfunding have enabled activists to reach wider audiences, mobilize supporters, and raise funds for environmental causes. Digital activism has also facilitated the rapid dissemination of information, allowing activists to respond quickly to environmental crises and build global movements.

However, the digital age also presents challenges for environmental activism. The spread of misinformation, the fragmentation of public discourse, and the surveillance and repression of activists by authoritarian governments are significant obstacles. Additionally, the digital divide means that not all communities have equal access to the tools of digital activism, potentially limiting the reach and effectiveness of environmental campaigns.

Building a Sustainable and Inclusive Movement: As environmental activism continues to evolve, it is increasingly focused on building a movement that is both sustainable and inclusive. This means addressing the intersections between environmental issues and social justice, ensuring that the voices of marginalized communities are heard, and recognizing the need for systemic change to achieve environmental sustainability.

The concept of "just transition," which seeks to ensure that the shift towards a sustainable economy is fair and equitable for all, has gained prominence within the environmental movement. Activists are working to ensure that workers in fossil fuel industries are not left behind in the transition to renewable energy and that vulnerable communities are protected from the impacts of environmental degradation.

Environmental activism must also contend with the challenge of maintaining momentum and public engagement in the face of long-term environmental challenges. Building a movement that can sustain itself over the decades required to address issues like climate change will require ongoing innovation, collaboration, and a commitment to justice and equity.

Conclusion

Environmental activism has played a crucial role in advancing the cause of environmental protection and sustainability. From grassroots organizing to global advocacy, activists have achieved significant victories in raising awareness, influencing policy, and holding powerful entities accountable for their environmental impact. However, the challenges facing the environmental movement are immense, particularly in the context of the climate crisis and the need for systemic change. As environmental activism continues to evolve, it will need to adapt to new realities, embrace a more inclusive and intersectional approach, and find ways to sustain its efforts in the face of ongoing environmental challenges. The future of the planet depends on the continued strength and resilience of the environmental movement.

Understanding Progressive and Wealth Taxation

Introduction

Progressive taxation is a system where the tax rate increases as the taxable income or wealth of an individual or entity increases. This approach contrasts with regressive and proportional taxation, where tax rates are the same or decrease relative to income. Progressive taxation is grounded in the principle of equity, aiming to reduce income inequality by ensuring that those with greater financial resources contribute a larger share to public revenue. In recent years, wealth taxation—a specific form of progressive taxation—has gained attention as a means of addressing the growing wealth gap. This analysis explores the concept of progressive taxation, its implementation, and the role of wealth taxes in modern economies.

1. The Concept and Principles of Progressive Taxation

The Structure of Progressive Taxation: In a progressive tax system, tax rates are divided into brackets, with higher rates applied to higher income or wealth levels. For example, in the United States, the federal income tax is progressive, with tax rates ranging from 10% for the lowest income bracket to 37% for the highest. As an individual's income increases, they move into higher tax brackets, paying a greater percentage of their income in taxes.

The key idea behind progressive taxation is that those with a greater ability to pay should contribute more to the funding of public goods and services, such as education, healthcare, infrastructure, and social security. This approach is based on the principle of vertical equity, which asserts that individuals with higher incomes should bear a larger portion of the tax burden to achieve a more equitable distribution of wealth and resources in society.

Economic and Social Justifications: Progressive taxation is often justified on both economic and social grounds. Economically, it is seen as a tool for reducing income inequality, which can have negative effects on social cohesion and economic stability. High levels of inequality can lead to reduced social mobility, increased crime rates, and political polarization. By redistributing wealth from the richest to the poorest, progressive taxation can help mitigate these negative outcomes and promote a more balanced and sustainable economy.

Socially, progressive taxation is viewed as a means of fostering social justice and fairness. It aligns with the idea that those who benefit the most from a country's economic system and infrastructure should contribute proportionally to its maintenance and improvement. This approach is seen as a way to ensure that all members of society have access to essential services and opportunities, regardless of their economic background.

Challenges and Criticisms: Despite its advantages, progressive taxation is not without challenges and criticisms. Opponents argue that high marginal tax rates can disincentivize work, savings, and investment, potentially leading to lower economic growth. There is also concern that complex progressive tax systems can create opportunities for tax avoidance and evasion, particularly among the wealthy who can afford sophisticated tax planning strategies.

Moreover, critics claim that progressive taxation can lead to government overreach and inefficiency, with public funds being misallocated or wasted. They advocate for flatter tax systems, which they argue are simpler, more transparent, and less likely to distort economic behavior.

Supporters of progressive taxation, however, counter that these concerns are often overstated. They argue that well-designed progressive tax systems can balance the need for revenue with the goal of economic efficiency, and that the social benefits of reducing inequality outweigh potential downsides.

2. Wealth Taxation as a Form of Progressive Taxation

Understanding Wealth Taxes: Wealth taxation is a type of progressive tax that targets the net wealth of individuals, rather than their income. A wealth tax is typically levied annually on the total value of an individual's assets, including real estate, stocks, bonds, and other forms of property, minus any debts or liabilities. Wealth taxes are designed to target the very wealthy, as a significant portion of wealth in modern economies is concentrated in the hands of a small percentage of the population.

Wealth taxes are seen as a way to address the limitations of income taxes in reducing economic inequality. While income taxes primarily target earnings from labor and investments, wealth taxes aim to directly reduce the concentration of wealth itself. This is particularly important in societies where wealth inequality is more pronounced than income inequality, with a large share of wealth being inherited rather than earned through work.

Arguments in Favor of Wealth Taxation: Proponents of wealth taxes argue that they are an effective tool for reducing extreme wealth disparities and generating revenue for public investment. By taxing wealth, governments can raise funds that can be used to improve social services, infrastructure, and public goods, benefiting society as a whole. Wealth taxes can also serve as a deterrent to the accumulation of excessive wealth, encouraging the wealthy to reinvest their assets in productive activities rather than hoarding them.

Wealth taxes are also seen as a way to address the growing concern that the wealthy are not paying their fair share of taxes. In many countries, the effective tax rate on the richest individuals has declined over time, as income from capital gains and dividends—which are often taxed at lower rates than ordinary income—makes up a larger share of their total income. Wealth taxes can help to correct this imbalance by ensuring that the wealthiest individuals contribute more to public finances.

Challenges and Criticisms of Wealth Taxes: Despite their potential benefits, wealth taxes face significant challenges and criticisms. One of the main concerns is the difficulty of accurately assessing and valuing wealth, particularly for assets that are not easily liquidated, such as real estate or closely held businesses. This can lead to disputes over valuations and create administrative burdens for both taxpayers and tax authorities.

Another criticism of wealth taxes is that they can lead to capital flight, where wealthy individuals move their assets or themselves to jurisdictions with lower or no wealth taxes. This can reduce the effectiveness of wealth taxes and potentially undermine the broader economy by reducing investment and economic activity.

Wealth taxes can also be politically contentious, as they often face strong opposition from wealthy individuals and interest groups who have significant influence over policymaking. In some countries, wealth taxes have been repealed or significantly weakened due to political pressure.

Examples of Wealth Taxation: Several countries have implemented wealth taxes, with varying degrees of success. In Europe, countries like France, Norway, and Switzerland have long-standing wealth taxes, though the design and impact of these taxes differ. For example, France's wealth tax was criticized for driving wealthy individuals out of the country and was eventually replaced with a tax on real estate wealth. In contrast, Switzerland's wealth tax has been more stable, benefiting from broad public support and effective administration.

In the United States, proposals for a federal wealth tax have gained traction in recent years, particularly among progressive politicians and policymakers. Senator Elizabeth Warren and Senator Bernie Sanders have both proposed wealth taxes as part of their platforms, arguing that such taxes are necessary to address the concentration of wealth and fund social programs. These proposals have sparked debate about the feasibility and desirability of wealth taxation in the U.S. context.

3. The Future of Progressive and Wealth Taxation

Policy Considerations: The future of progressive and wealth taxation will depend on a range of factors, including political dynamics, economic conditions, and public opinion. As income and wealth inequality continue to rise in many parts of the world, there may be increasing pressure on governments to adopt more progressive tax policies, including wealth taxes.

For progressive and wealth taxation to be effective, policymakers will need to carefully consider the design and implementation of these taxes. This includes ensuring that tax rates are set at levels that balance revenue generation with economic efficiency, minimizing opportunities for tax avoidance, and addressing the administrative challenges of assessing and collecting wealth taxes.

Global Coordination: Given the global nature of wealth and capital flows, there is also a growing recognition of the need for international coordination on tax policy. Without such coordination, efforts to tax the wealthy could be undermined by tax havens and other jurisdictions with low or no wealth taxes. Initiatives like the OECD's efforts to establish global tax standards and crack down on tax evasion and avoidance are steps in this direction.

Social Implications: The debate over progressive and wealth taxation also has important social implications. These taxes are not just about raising revenue; they are also about addressing broader questions of fairness, equity, and the role of government in society. As such, the conversation about progressive taxation is likely to continue, reflecting deeper concerns about the distribution of wealth and power in modern economies.

Conclusion

Progressive taxation, including wealth taxation, remains a key tool for addressing economic inequality and ensuring that those with the greatest financial resources contribute their fair share to the common good. While these taxes face significant challenges and criticisms, they are grounded in principles of equity and social justice that resonate with many people. As societies grapple with the challenges of rising inequality and the need for public investment, the role of progressive and wealth taxation is likely to remain a central issue in economic and political debates.

Universal Basic Income: An Overview

Introduction

Universal Basic Income (UBI) is a policy proposal that has gained significant attention in recent years as a potential solution to various social and economic challenges. The concept of UBI involves providing all citizens with a regular, unconditional cash payment regardless of their income, employment status, or wealth. Advocates argue that UBI can reduce poverty, address income inequality, and provide financial security in an era of rapid technological change and economic uncertainty. However, the idea of UBI is also met with skepticism and criticism, particularly regarding its feasibility, cost, and potential impact on work incentives. This analysis explores the concept of UBI, its historical roots, the arguments for and against it, and the experiments and discussions surrounding its implementation.

1. The Concept and Historical Roots of Universal Basic Income

Definition and Key Features: Universal Basic Income is a form of social security in which all citizens receive a regular, unconditional sum of money from the government. The key features of UBI include its universality, meaning it is available to everyone regardless of their financial situation; its regularity, as payments are made on a consistent basis (monthly or annually); and its unconditionality, meaning there are no requirements to receive the payment, such as employment or means-testing.

The amount of money provided through UBI is intended to cover basic living expenses, such as food, shelter, and clothing, allowing individuals to meet their essential needs without the pressure of having to secure employment. The idea is that by providing a guaranteed income floor, UBI can empower individuals to make choices that improve their quality of life, such as pursuing education, starting a business, or engaging in creative or caregiving activities.

Historical Origins: The concept of UBI is not new; it has deep historical roots that can be traced back to various thinkers and movements throughout history. One of the earliest proponents of a basic income was the English philosopher Thomas More, who in his 1516 book *Utopia* proposed that all citizens should receive a guaranteed income to reduce theft and poverty.

In the 18th century, the American revolutionary Thomas Paine advocated for a form of basic income in his pamphlet *Agrarian Justice* (1797), where he proposed that all citizens receive a stipend funded by a tax on landowners to address poverty and inequality. Similarly, the French economist and philosopher Charles Fourier in the early 19th century supported the idea of providing all citizens with a minimum income to ensure their basic needs were met.

Throughout the 20th century, the idea of UBI continued to gain traction among various political and economic thinkers, including economist Milton Friedman, who proposed a "negative income tax" as a means of ensuring a minimum income for all. The negative income tax concept, while different in implementation, shares similarities with UBI in that it aims to provide financial support to those with low or no income.

Modern Interest and Experiments: In the 21st century, UBI has gained renewed interest as technological advancements, particularly in automation and artificial intelligence, have raised concerns about job displacement and the future of work. The rise of the gig economy, increasing income inequality, and the limitations of existing welfare systems have further fueled discussions about the potential benefits of UBI.

Several countries and regions have conducted or are conducting experiments with UBI to test its feasibility and impact. Notable examples include Finland, which ran a two-year UBI pilot from 2017 to 2018, providing

2,000 unemployed individuals with a monthly payment; and the city of Stockton, California, which launched a basic income experiment in 2019, providing 125 residents with $500 er month.

These experiments have provided valuable insights into the effects of UBI on employment, well-being, and social outcomes, though the results are often mixed and context-dependent.

2. Arguments for and Against Universal Basic Income

Arguments in Favor of UBI:

1. Poverty Reduction and Economic Security:
Proponents of UBI argue that it is an effective tool for reducing poverty and providing economic security, especially in a world where traditional employment is becoming less stable. By ensuring that everyone has access to a basic income, UBI can help to alleviate poverty, reduce reliance on welfare programs, and provide a safety net for those who are unable to work due to illness, disability, or other factors.

2. Freedom and Autonomy:
UBI is seen as a way to enhance individual freedom and autonomy. With a guaranteed income, people have more choices about how to live their lives, including the ability to pursue education, start a business, or engage

in caregiving or volunteer work without the pressure of needing to earn a living. This increased freedom can lead to greater personal fulfillment and social well-being.

3. Simplification of Welfare Systems:

Another argument in favor of UBI is that it can simplify existing welfare systems by replacing a complex web of means-tested benefits with a single, universal payment. This could reduce administrative costs, eliminate the stigma associated with welfare, and ensure that everyone receives support regardless of their circumstances.

4. Economic Stimulus:

UBI can act as an economic stimulus by putting money directly into the hands of consumers, who are likely to spend it on goods and services. This increased demand can help to boost the economy, particularly during times of recession or economic downturn.

5. Addressing Technological Unemployment:

As automation and artificial intelligence continue to advance, there is growing concern that many jobs will be replaced by machines, leading to widespread unemployment. UBI is seen as a potential solution to this problem, providing financial support to those displaced by technology and allowing them to transition to new forms of work or retraining.

Arguments Against UBI:

1. Cost and Feasibility:
One of the most significant criticisms of UBI is its cost. Providing every citizen with a basic income would require substantial public spending, which opponents argue could lead to higher taxes, increased government debt, or cuts to other essential services. Critics also question whether UBI is the most efficient use of public funds, especially in comparison to targeted welfare programs.

2. Work Incentives:
Critics of UBI argue that it could reduce work incentives, leading to lower labor force participation and potentially harming the economy. They suggest that if people receive a guaranteed income without needing to work, some may choose to work less or not at all, which could reduce productivity and economic growth.

3. Inflation and Economic Distortions:
There is concern that UBI could lead to inflation, as increased consumer spending could drive up prices for goods and services. Additionally, opponents argue that UBI could create economic distortions by encouraging

people to leave the workforce, leading to labor shortages in certain industries.

4. Equity Concerns:

While UBI is intended to promote equity, some critics argue that it could actually exacerbate inequality if the payments are not sufficient to meet the needs of the poorest individuals or if the funding mechanism is regressive. They suggest that targeted welfare programs may be more effective in addressing specific needs and reducing inequality.

5. Political and Social Resistance:

Finally, the implementation of UBI faces significant political and social resistance. Many people are skeptical of the idea of providing money without conditions, and there is concern that UBI could undermine the work ethic or foster a sense of entitlement. Additionally, existing welfare programs and interest groups may resist the shift to a UBI system, fearing loss of influence or funding.

3. The Future of Universal Basic Income

The Path Forward: The future of UBI depends on various factors, including economic conditions, political will, and public support. While UBI has gained traction in academic and policy circles, its implementation on a large scale remains uncertain. Continued experimentation and research will be essential to understanding the potential benefits and drawbacks of UBI, as well as identifying the most effective ways to design and fund such a program.

Policy Considerations: If UBI is to be implemented, policymakers will need to carefully consider several key issues, including the amount of the payment, the funding mechanism, and the interaction with existing welfare programs. They will also need to address concerns about work incentives, inflation, and economic inequality, ensuring that UBI is part of a broader strategy to promote social and economic justice.

Global Perspectives: The debate over UBI is global, with different countries and regions exploring the concept in various ways. While the specific design and implementation of UBI may vary depending on local conditions, the underlying principles of economic security, freedom, and equity resonate with people around the world. As such, UBI is likely to remain a topic of discussion and experimentation in the years to come.

Conclusion

Universal Basic Income is a bold and ambitious policy proposal that seeks to address some of the most pressing social and economic challenges of our time. By providing a guaranteed income to all citizens, UBI has the potential to reduce poverty, enhance individual freedom, and provide economic security in an era of rapid change. However, the implementation of UBI faces significant challenges, including concerns about cost, work incentives, and political feasibility. As discussions about UBI continue, it is essential to weigh the potential benefits against the challenges and to consider how UBI can be part of a broader strategy for creating a more just and equitable society.

Thank you.
August, 2024

www.ingramcontent.com/pod-product-compliance
Lightning Source LLC
Chambersburg PA
CBHW051552250726
48653CB00004BA/1116